Postcard Impressions of Early 20th-Century Singapore

Postcard Impressions
of Early 20th-Century Singapore

Perspectives from the Japanese Community

From the Lim Shao Bin Collection, National Library Singapore

Regina Hong, Ling Xi Min and Naoko Shimazu

 National Library Board Singapore

 Marshall Cavendish Editions

Writers: Regina Hong, Ling Xi Min and Naoko Shimazu
Project Team: Stephanie Pee, Gracie Lee, Lim Shao Bin, Wong Siok Muoi
Editorial Consultant: Francis Dorai
Design and Production: Marshall Cavendish International (Asia)
Printer: Times Printers

Published by:
National Library Board, Singapore
100 Victoria Street
#14-01 National Library Building
Singapore 188064
email: ref@nlb.gov.sg
www.nlb.gov.sg

National Library Board, Singapore Cataloguing in Publication Data

Names: Hong, Regina, author. | Ling, Xi Min, author. | Shimazu, Naoko, author.
Title: Postcard impressions of early 20th-century Singapore : perspectives from the Japanese community / Regina Hong, Ling Xi Min and Naoko Shimazu.
Description: Singapore : National Library Board/Marshall Cavendish, [2020] | From the Lim Shao Bin Collection, National Library Singapore.
Identifier(s). OCN 1141872843 | ISBN 978-981-14-2706-0 (hardcover)
Subject(s): LCSH: Postcards--Singapore--History--20th century. | Japanese--Singapore--History--20th century. | Singapore--History--20th century.
Classification: DDC 959.57--dc23

Front endpaper image (see page 65): Scene from a postcard showing a fishing village in the waters off Pulau Brani, a scene that travellers would have encountered as their ships pulled into Singapore's harbour. *Accession no.: B32413807F_0001*

Back endpaper image (see page 58): This postcard features the Central Police Station on South Bridge Road in Singapore (top left) as well as the vessel S.S. *Sanuki Maru* of the NYK (bottom right). *Accession no.: B32413805D_0093*

Contents

Foreword

The picture postcard's heyday was in the late 19th to early 20th centuries. It was a quick and easy way to communicate – whatever one wanted to write was confined to a small blank space – that also doubled as a keepsake of one's travels. Compact in size and convenient to post, old postcards have become collector's items today, valued for the rare images, stamps and postmarks they contain, and oftentimes for the messages and identities of the senders and addressees.

Postcards, such as the ones found in the Lim Shao Bin Collection at the National Library, can also illuminate history, in this instance providing a rare glimpse into the origins, practices and culture of the Japanese community in Singapore during the pre-war period. While much has been written about the Japanese Occupation in Singapore, we know a lot less about the Japanese who resided here prior to the Second World War.

The postcards showcased in this publication feature international shipping routes that point to Singapore's place in the global trade network, as well as landmarks and scenes of a bygone era. The writers – Regina Hong and Ling Xi Min, together with Professor Naoko Shimazu from Yale-NUS College in Singapore – have put together a selection of postcards from the collection that not only help us understand the lives of the early Japanese settlers who sank their roots on this island, but also provide fascinating perspectives of early Japanese travellers passing through Singapore.

This study would not have been possible without the postcards that Mr Lim Shao Bin, an independent researcher who has been collecting Japanese historical materials for the last 30 years, kindly donated to the National Library. Beyond postcards, the collection also contains important Japanese maps and atlases, newspapers, books and documents, mostly relating to the Second World War in Singapore and Southeast Asia. We are grateful to Mr Lim, who shared his vast knowledge and expertise with the writers, often pointing to the significance of specific elements on the postcards.

I hope that *Postcard Impressions of Early 20th-Century Singapore* will encourage further research into our collections and enable people to discover little-known aspects of Singapore's fascinating and multi-faceted history.

Tan Huism
Director, National Library, Singapore

CARTE

POSTALE

INTRODUCTION

POSTCARD VIEWS

The picture postcards in the Lim Shao Bin Collection at the National Library offer fascinating insights into Singapore society in the late 19th and early 20th centuries. Many of the postcards in this collection are Japanese in origin, providing interesting historical perspectives on early Japanese connections to the island, as recorded by Japanese travellers and overseas Japanese living in Singapore, as well as Japanese photographers and publishers operating in Singapore before the Second World War.

Used as a vehicle for advertisement, personal correspondence, souvenirs and even propaganda, the picture postcard has taken on many roles throughout history. Due to their popularity and accessibility, postcards can be important primary sources of information. Unfortunately, there is precious little English-language scholarship on Japanese postcards outside the contexts of war and empire, and even less research done on the postcards used by the Japanese community in Singapore before 1941.

As a historical document, the picture postcard is an interesting format; it not only provides visual clues (for example, one can draw insights from the scenes that are typically represented on postcards), but also important textual information about its writer and historical context.

Given the size of the postcards, however, the messages they contain tend to be brief and fragmentary, making it a challenge to obtain detailed information about their senders and recipients. Therefore, careful attention should be paid not only to the written messages but also other clues, such as addresses, printed images and illustrations, publisher details, as well as stamps and postmarks – all these can expand our understanding beyond what is conveyed by the written text alone.

While there has been substantial research on Japan's involvement in Singapore during the Second World War, much less is known about the social history of the Japanese community residing on the island before the war. This book hopes to plug that gap by examining the Japanese postcards in the Lim Shao Bin Collection along three thematic angles: illustrated maps on postcards, tourism, and the lives of Japanese subjects residing in early Singapore. It also hopes to shed light on how Japanese postcards were produced and circulated in Singapore, a topic that has not been the subject of much study.

In this book, the term "postcards" refers to picture postcards, unless otherwise stated. "Japanese postcards" are broadly defined as: postcards featuring Japanese subject matter; postcards produced in Japan or by Japanese photographic studios, printers and stationers in Singapore and Malaya; and/or postcards bearing Japanese-language messages. Apart from these, a number of postcards from the Lim Shao Bin Collection that do not fit these categories have been included to illustrate certain points. As a first step, we shall explore briefly the use and production of postcards in Singapore during the late 19th and early 20th centuries.

Postcards in Pre-World War II Singapore

The postcard was developed as a result of innovations in the global postal system during the mid-19th century. The first official postcards in Singapore, which came printed with the stamp, were issued by the Straits Settlements government (see PC1) in 1879 (see table overleaf for postal rates).[1] Privately issued postcards were not as popular as they were charged at the same rate as a normal letter, meaning they could cost twice as much as official postcards to send.[2] This changed 15 years later in 1894, when British postal authorities amended their policies to allow private postcards to be posted at the same rate as official ones.[3]

By the 1900s, the sale of private picture postcards had become a profitable business, prompting many international and local publishing firms to enter the market.[4] In his 1905 report, the Postmaster-General in Singapore, Noel Trotter, noted that the large increase in the number of postcards handled were due to the rise in popularity of picture postcards, attesting to the rapid growth of the postcard industry.[5]

PRICES OF GOVERNMENT-ISSUED POSTCARDS IN 1879

Stamp value	Route	Price
3 cents	Via Brindisi (when not forwarded through Great Britain) or for transmission via Marseille, Southampton, or any other route to countries belonging to the Postal Union	35 cents per packet of 10 postcards
4 cents	Via Brindisi to the United Kingdom and to countries belonging to the Postal Union beyond Great Britain	45 cents per packet of 10 postcards

These postcards could be purchased at the General Post Office in Singapore or at the post offices of Penang and Melaka. Stamp vendors were also allowed to sell these cards individually and could charge "for each a cent more than the value of the stamp indicated on the [c]ard".

Source: Government notification No. 360. [Microfilm: NL 1009]. (1879, September 26). *Straits Settlements Government Gazette*. Singapore: Government Printing Office, p. 871. (Call no.: RRARE 959.57 SGG)

PRICES OF COMMERCIAL POSTCARDS IN 1906

Seller	Details	Price
Jitts & Co.	Singapore souvenir postcards featuring five different views of decorations put up on the occasion of H.R.H. Prince Arthur of Connaught's visit	25 cents per packet
Kim & Co.	Local cards in 100 varieties (coloured and uncoloured) Note: The source states that coloured cards were priced at 3 cents and uncoloured ones at 5 cents. This might have been a typographical error as coloured cards were likely to have cost more.	3 cents (uncoloured) 5 cents (coloured)
C.A. Ribeiro & Co.	Photographic postcards featuring landscapes and types of Singapore (24 different kinds)	15 cents each or $1.50 per dozen

Sources: Jitts & Co.: Advertisements Column 3. [Microfilm: NL 2977]. (1906, September 6). *Eastern Daily Mail and Straits Morning Advertiser*, p. 1.; Kim & Co.: Advertisements Column 1. [Microfilm: NL 2977]. (1906, September 20). *Eastern Daily Mail and Straits Morning Advertiser*, p. 2.; C.A. Ribeiro & Co.: Advertisements Column 1. [Microfilm: NL 2977]. (1906, September 20). *Eastern Daily Mail and Straits Morning Advertiser*, p. 2.

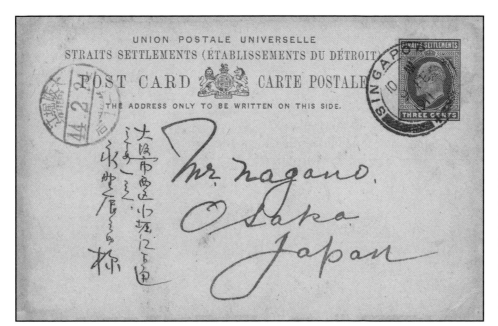

UNION POSTALE UNIVERSELLE
STRAITS SETTLEMENTS (ÉTABLISSEMENTS DU DÉTROIT)
POST CARD   CARTE POSTALE
THE ADDRESS ONLY TO BE WRITTEN ON THIS SIDE.

SINGAPORE

STRAITS SETTLEMENTS
THREE CENTS

大阪市西区小坂12ノ5通
永野信三
様

Mr. Nagano.
Osaka
Japan

PC1
This postcard is an example of the official postcards first issued by the Straits Settlements government. This postcard was sent to a Mr Nagano in Osaka, Japan, in 1911. *Produced by the Straits Settlements. Postmarked 9 February 1911. Accession no: B32413805D_0006*

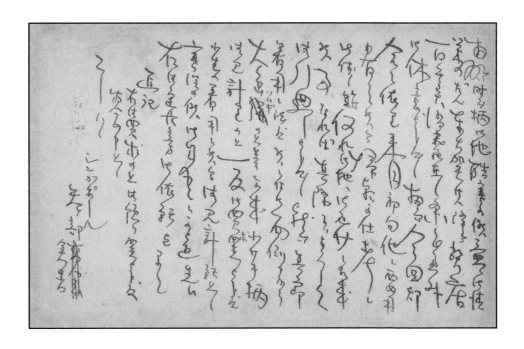

Other factors that contributed to this growth included the affordability of privately printed picture postcards and the relatively inexpensive postal rates for mailing postcards. In addition, the increase in the number of international travellers due to the opening of the Suez Canal in 1869 – with Singapore being a key port of call along many major shipping routes – also fuelled a corresponding demand for picture postcards as souvenirs.

Competitions organised for collectors to showcase their pieces reflected the growth of the postcard industry. In 1908, Koh & Co., one of the biggest sellers of postcards in Singapore at the time, announced a "competitive exhibition" of picture postcards to encourage collectors to present their best pieces. Each collector could submit up to 500 postcards, with 14 prizes up for grabs.[6] The competition drew eight participants from Singapore and Malaysia and was held at Raffles Hotel from 4 to 6 February 1909.[7] Koh &

KOH & CO.'S COMPETITIVE EXHIBITION OF POSTCARDS

One of the rules of this competitive exhibition required each postcard submitted to have passed through the General Post Office in Singapore. H.T. Jensen of G.R. Lambert & Co. (a local photography studio) and Lee Keng Yan (also spelt Lee Kiag Yan), a local Chinese photographer from Chop Koon Sun (possibly the studio or company he worked at), presided as judges and awarded the prizes to:

1st   Lee Kim San (Singapore) who received a silver medal and an album "for a collection which, while being excellent, embraced the widest variety"

2nd   Daphne Richards (Singapore) who received a medal and an album "for a remarkably fine selection, that however, lacked wide variety"

3rd   Chia Tiong Kim (Singapore) who received a medal "for a very good collection"

4th   Cyril Kwa (Kuala Lumpur) who received a medal

Source: Novel postcard exhibition. [Microfilm: NL 316]. (1908, September 22). *The Straits Times*, p. 8.; Postcard exhibition. [Microfilm: NL 318]. (1909, February 4). *The Straits Times*, p. 7.

Co. also published a monthly journal, thought to have begun in 1907, called the *Postcard Exchange Register*.[8]

Some of the postcards for sale in Singapore at the time were imported from countries such as Britain and Japan. Those produced in Japan not only featured scenes of Japan but also Singapore scenes and landmarks – such as Victoria Memorial Hall (see PC51 and PC52 in Chapter 2) and Raffles Hotel (see PC68 in Chapter 2) – as well as industries such as rubber cultivation (see PC36j and PC41 in Chapter 2).

During the First World War, postcards were sold in Singapore to raise funds in support of the British Empire's war effort. The London firm Raphael Tuck and Sons Ltd. was commissioned to produce two series of postcards, *Our Navy and Army* and *Defenders of the Empire*, in aid of the Prince of Wales' National Relief Fund. These postcards were in turn consigned to Koh & Co. for distribution and sale in Singapore, as shown in Figure 1.[9]

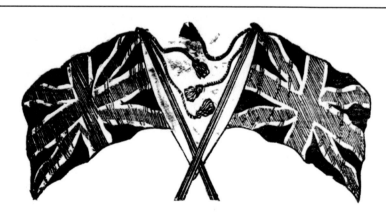

PATRIOTIC POSTCARDS.

A very large collection of Tuck's Postcards of Our Navy and Army Series showing the pictures of All the Dreadnoughts and Cruisers and All the "Famous Men in the Army" giving every detail on each postcard, also "Defenders of the Empire" series. (Published by Raphael Tuck and Sons, Ltd., by special request in Aid of the Prince of Wales' National Relief Fund.)

KOH & Co., Booksellers, Stationers & News Agents, 82-3 Bras Basah Road.

Figure 1
Advertisement by Koh & Co. promoting the postcard series, *Our Navy and Army* and *Defenders of the Empire*.

Source: Untitled. [Microfilm: NL 2094]. (1915, June 2). *Malaya Tribune*, p. 4.

Apart from imported postcards, there were also those issued by private local photography studios. Established in 1867, G.R. Lambert & Co. was possibly one of the most well-known photography studios at the time.[10] The studio was appointed as photographers to the King of Siam (Thailand) and Sultan of Johor, and was renowned for its high-quality photographs that were "of an excellence difficult to surpass".[11]

Wilson & Co. was another major picture postcard publisher. The company was appointed to produce postcards for Hotel de l'Europe (located where the National Gallery Singapore now stands), which were distributed as advertising collateral or tourist mementos. Some commonly featured scenes on Wilson and Co.'s postcards include traditional houses, *sampans* and fishing villages in Singapore (PC2, as well as PC37 and PC38 in Chapter 2).

Rural scenes such as those in PC2 were typically depicted on postcards produced in Singapore at the time. Many of the postcards sold at the turn of the 20th century presented aspects of native life in a bid to appeal to European consumers and their acquaintances back home.[12] These scenes of everyday life in Singapore may have seemed quite ordinary to local residents, but for overseas consumers they represented a slice of the exotic and mysterious Orient.

However, Europeans were not the only ones who purchased these cards. Japanese consumers bought and used these cards as *nengajō*, or New Year's greeting cards, as seen in PC2 (see PC117–120 in Chapter 4, which also includes a discussion of the *nengajō* circulated by the Japanese community in Singapore).

Postcards in Japanese Culture

As the Japanese community in Singapore grew, they brought with them a rich postcard culture. In order to understand the place of Japanese postcards in pre-WWII Singapore, we must first look at the ways in which postcards have been traditionally viewed and used in Japan.

In 1875, the first official Japanese postcards were issued by the Meiji government (1868–1912); it took another 25 years, in 1900, before commercial postcards by private publishers were officially accepted for use.[13]

In the early 20th century, picture postcards in Japan became highly coveted collector's items, spurred by the fervour over commemorative postcards of the

PC2
Posting a *nengajō*, or New Year's card, was a tradition in Japan. This postcard, featuring a Malay village in Singapore, was addressed to a Mr Yamazaki in Nagano, Japan.
Postmarked 1910 (Meiji 43rd year). Published by Wilson & Co. for Hotel de l'Europe & Orchard Road, Singapore. Accession no.: B32413805D_0059

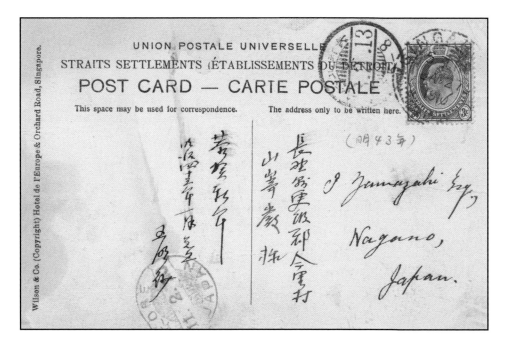

Russo-Japanese War (1904–5). Some of the finest postcards from this period can be distinguished by their highly artistic and ornate features (such as gold stamping and embossing). They were produced to commemorate war victories (see PC3), and were avidly collected by enthusiasts both at home and on the battlefields. Soldiers writing home frequently used postcards and their friends in turn would send picture postcards of beautiful women (*bijin*) to motivate them while they were at the frontlines.[14] On the peripheries of the war zone, a trade on postcards of "Japanese beauties" boomed, including some featuring pornographic content, usually of Japanese Red Cross nurses.[15]

By 1904–5, picture postcards arguably supplanted the demand for Japanese brocade prints, known as *nishikie*, which were popular collectables during the First Sino-Japanese War (1894–5). In some ways, picture postcards represented a new approachability to art – a fresh form of consumable, affordable art that was accessible to everyone. This rising popularity of picture postcards as art may have been linked to the Japanese pastime of ink-brush painting known as *fude-e*, an art form still practised in Japan today, on blank postcards.

Themes Presented on Japanese Postcards

The shift from the Meiji (1868–1912) to Taisho era (1912–25) saw an increase in the variety of themes and subject matter presented on picture postcards. Apart from modern concepts such as new culture homes (*bunka jūtaku*)[16] and themes such as the empowerment of women, the picture postcards also featured scenes from Japan's overseas territories like Taiwan and Saipan.[17]

Picture postcards of these colonies rarely featured the Japanese communities living there. Rather, they bore images of local buildings, people and food to satisfy the curious gaze of the Japanese.[18] For the Japanese in Japan, these postcards chronicled their nation's expanding empire, while for the Japanese traveller or migrant living abroad, these postcards served as a means of sharing scenes from a foreign land with friends and family back home (see PC4).

Although postcards imported from Japan were widely available in Singapore, postcards containing objectionable subject matter, namely pornographic content, that were permissible in Japan were restricted for sale or display in Singapore. This was a

PC3
Postcards were often used to commemorate Japan's war victories, and in this instance, the Battle of Port Arthur during the Russo-Japanese War. Captioned "The Seventy Seven Heroes Who Resolved to Fight until Death Bravery [sic] Attempted to Block Port Arthur", this postcard was sent from Singapore to Paris, France. This postcard is also an official Universal Postal Union (UPU) postcard, published by the Japan Post Office.
Postmarked 8 May 1905.
Publisher: Japan Post Office. Accession no.: B32413805D_0029

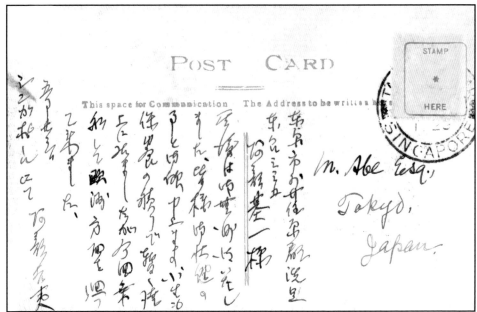

PC4
This postcard features a group of villagers in traditional Malay dress. Japanese travellers would send postcards featuring scenes such as this back home as a way of sharing their experiences abroad. In this card, the writer conveys his general greetings and notes that he is fine in Singapore.
Date and publisher unknown.
Accession no.: B29626253B_0047

crucial difference in commercial regulations that some Japanese postcard sellers and producers claimed they were unaware of. As a result, some of these postcards featuring "Japanese beauties" made their way to Singapore, with some even produced locally for sale. The British colonial authorities in Singapore, however, took offence to these lewd postcards and slapped their purveyors with heavy fines and, in some instances, even destroyed the offending postcards.[19]

Overview of the Chapters

This book explores Japanese impressions, perspectives, experiences and representations of Singapore through postcards. What themes can we find in these postcards? How were they used? What can they tell us about the people who used them?[20]

Chapter 1 examines picture postcards that depict maps, with a particular focus on those that feature Singapore. These postcards were important not only for conveying information to potential customers about the major shipping routes and the arrival and departure times of vessels, but also allowed families of migrants to trace their loved ones' journeys to faraway new lands. When Singapore fell in 1942 during the Second World War, however, these postcards took on a darker, more ominous meaning when maps began to feature Singapore as a conquered territory.

Chapter 2 explores how Singapore was perceived by Japanese travellers stopping over on their way to Europe. What did these tourists do here? Which places did they visit? The postcards that these travellers mailed out and the messages they wrote not only give us insight into Singapore as a tourist destination, but also valuable information about its budding tourism industry.

In Chapter 3, we look at the pre-war Japanese community.[21] Who were the Japanese living in Singapore? How did they feel about living in an unfamiliar place? How were they perceived by other ethnic communities in Singapore? This chapter attempts to provide a brief account of the pre-war Japanese presence in Singapore as a lead-up to the final chapter, which explores how postcards were produced and used by the local Japanese community.

The final chapter moves away from postcards as historical sources to the social history of these postcards. What was the history behind the production of these postcards? How were they used? Beyond personal correspondence, picture postcards were also used as souvenirs, commemoratives and mementos. Today, postcards are not merely collector's items but also valuable records of history. Sometimes, postcards may even be the only historical record of a time that has largely faded from memory.

Appended at the end of each chapter are supplementary postcards from the Lim Shao Bin Collection. These postcards provide a sense of the breadth and variety of postcards that are available in the collection.

POSTCARD STYLISTICS

Generally, there are two ways to determine a Japanese postcard's date of publication:

1   Postcard design
    - Undivided-back (1900–07)
    - Divided-back: one third of postcard's reverse side allocated for correspondence (1907–19)
    - Divided-back: half of postcard's reverse side allocated for correspondence (1919 onwards)

2   Characters printed on the reverse side of the postcard
    - はかき郵便 *hakaki yūbin* (before 1933)
    - はがき郵便 *hagaki yūbin* (1933 onwards)

Source: 学習院大学資料館 [Gakushūin daigaku shiryōkan]. (2012). *絵葉書で読み解く大正時代* [Ehagaki de yomitoku Taishō jidai]. Tokyo, Japan: Sairyūsha, p. 8. (Not available in NLB holdings)

About the Collection

The Lim Shao Bin Collection features materials donated to the National Library Board, Singapore by Mr Lim Shao Bin. Mr Lim, an independent history researcher, started collecting Japanese historical materials on Singapore and Southeast Asia in the 1980s when he was working and studying in Japan. Although Mr Lim returned to Singapore to work later, he managed to amass over 1,500 items, including more than 600 picture postcards, over a 30-year period.[22] Most of the materials are in Japanese and date from the mid-Meiji to early Showa eras.

The postcards featured in this publication were purchased by Mr Lim while he was in Japan; some were formerly in the possession of Japanese families, and were still in their original packaging when he acquired them. While most of these picture postcards feature familiar landmarks in Singapore, such as St Andrew's Cathedral and the Church of the Good Shepherd (elevated to the status of a Cathedral in 1888), there are also postcards of less recognisable places, like the Japanese hotel Koyokan, that have since been lost to time, making this collection an important visual record of vanishing landscapes in Singapore.

Besides picture postcards, the Lim Shao Bin Collection also holds Japanese maps and atlases of Southeast Asia from the 1860s to 2000s; letters and other correspondence that offer insights into the social networks and lives of Japanese residents in Singapore; as well as books, newspapers, ephemera and periodicals relating to the Second World War. Mr Lim donated these rare materials to the National Library Board between 2016 and 2020 in order to encourage research and scholarship into an important period of Singapore's multifaceted history.[23]

Notes

1   Cheah, J. S. (2006). *Singapore: 500 Early Postcards*. Singapore: Editions Didier Millet, p. 8. (Call no.: RSING 769.566095957 CHE)

2   The cost of sending a letter not exceeding an ounce (approximately 14 grams) was 8 or 12 cents, depending on destination. National Archives. (2014). *Singapore Historical Postcards*. Singapore: Marshall Cavendish Editions, p. 8. (The 1986 edition is available at Call no.: RSING 769.95957 SIN); Straits Settlements [Microfilm: NL 1009]. (1879, April 4) *Straits Settlements Government Gazette*, Singapore: Government Printing Office, p. 246.; Straits Settlements [Microfilm: NL 1009]. (1879, September 26). *Straits Settlements Government Gazette*, p. 871.

3   National Archives, 2014, p. 8.

4   National Archives, 2014, p. 10.

5   Annual report on the Postal and Telegraph Department of the Straits Settlements for the year 1905. [Microfilm: NL 1059]. (1906, July 27). Supplement to the *Straits Settlements Government Gazette*, No. 46. Singapore: Government Printing Office, p. 1. (Call no.: RRARE 959.51 SGG); Makepeace, W. (1991). *One hundred years of Singapore*. Singapore: Oxford University Press, p. 162. (Call no.: RSING 959.57 ONE –[HIS])

6   Novel postcard exhibition. [Microfilm: NL 316]. (1908, September 22). *The Straits Times*, p. 8.

7   Postcard exhibition. [Microfilm: NL 318]. (1909, February 4). *The Straits Times*, p. 7.; Advertisements Column 5. [Microfilm: NL 318]. (1909, February 5). *The Straits Times*, p. 10.

8   Cheah, 2006, p. 11.

9   Advertisements Column 2. [Microfilm: NL 2094]. (1915, June 2). *Malaya Tribune*, p. 4.

10 Notice [Microfilm: NL 5217]. (1867, April 11). *The Singapore Daily Times*, p. 2.

11 Coming art exhibition. [Microfilm: NL 2975]. (1906, February 1). *Eastern Daily Mail and Straits Morning Advertiser*, p. 2.

12 Scenes of 'native life' decorated greeting cards. [Microfilm: NL 16863]. (1989, November 26). *The Straits Times*, p. 2.

13 学習院大学資料館 [Gakushūin daigaku shiryōkan]. (2012). 絵葉書で読み解く大正時代 [Ehagaki de yomitoku Taishō jidai]. Tokyo, Japan: Sairyūsha, pp. 7, 11. (Not available in NLB holdings)

14 Gakushūin daigaku shiryōkan, 2012, p. 5.

15 Shimazu, N. (2009). *Japanese Society at War: Death, Memory and the Russo-Japanese War*. Cambridge: Cambridge University Press, pp. 89–90. (Call no.: R 952.031 SHI)

16 *Bunka jūtaku* was a new kind of residential building built in the later half of the Taisho period. Although these houses featured European design elements on the exterior, the interior chiefly comprised Japanese architectural features.

17 Gakushūin daigaku shiryōkan, 2012, p. 65, 101.

18 Gakushūin daigaku shiryōkan, 2012, p. 65.

19 Untitled. [Microfilm: NL 507]. (1923, June 19). *The Straits Times*, p. 8.; Untitled. [Microfilm: NL 513]. (1923, December 18). *The Straits Times*, p. 8.; A business in obscene postcards. [Microfilm: NL 1991]. (1930, January 1). *The Singapore Free Press and Mercantile Advertiser*, p. 16.

20 Japanese names will be presented with last names first, unless otherwise specified in the original.

21 In this book, pre-war refers to the period between the arrival of the first official Japanese migrant in 1862 to just before the Japanese Occupation of Singapore in 1942.

22 Lim is also the author of *Images of Singapore from the Japanese perspective* [published in 2004 by The Japanese Cultural Society (Call no.: RSING 959.57 IMA)], a book that contains over 1,000 images from postcards, maps and photo albums that trace shifting Japanese perspectives of Singapore.

23 For more information on the Lim Shao Bin Collection, please see: Lee, G. (July, 2018). "Japan in Southeast Asia: The Lim Shao Bin Collection", in *BiblioAsia* 14(2). Singapore: National Library Board, Singapore. Retrieved from BiblioAsia website. Selected materials from the collection can be viewed at PictureSG and at Archives Online.

CHAPTER 1

MAPPING THE WORLD
ON POSTCARDS

In the early 20th century, ships were a key mode of transportation for people and goods between Japan and the rest of the world. Shipping routes spanned impressive distances from Tokyo to Europe via Singapore and the Suez Canal. This is why early Japanese postcards often featured illustrations of maps as well as shipping routes. Apart from their aesthetic value, these postcards also served other practical purposes: as advertisements for shipping companies; as useful sources of information on travelling routes for the families of economic migrants; and as a means for public engagement by the Imperial Japanese Navy and propaganda for the Imperial Japanese Army during the Second World War.

Postcards with illustrations of maps and shipping routes enabled the Japanese public to visualise and imagine a world beyond their homeland. A study of these postcards also reveals how deeply connected Singapore was with the global transport networks of the late 19th to 20th centuries.

Shipping Routes

Maps and shipping routes were highly popular subjects for postcards issued by shipping companies, whose vessels often carried both passengers and cargo. Nippon Yūsen Kaisha (Japan Mail Steamship Company) and Osaka Commercial Corporation were two such firms. Their postcards often depicted detailed drawings of shipping routes, with the names of ports and expected dates of arrival (PC5 and PC6). These postcards indicate that Singapore was an important port lying on major international shipping

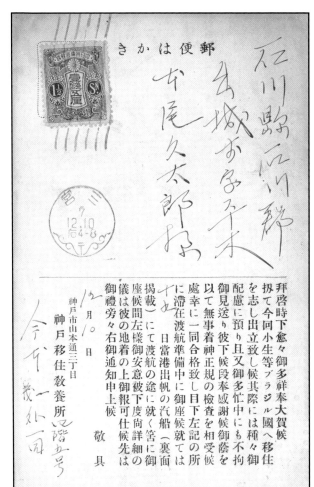

PC5

This postcard features the *Buenos Aires-maru*, a steamer in the O.S.K. Lines (Osaka Shōsen Kaisha) shipping fleet. Singapore (written in *katakana*, pronounced as "Shingapōru") is listed as the third port of call and expected to arrive on the "12th day after departure". The pre-printed message notes that the sender of the postcard has completed all the necessary procedures for emigration to Brazil and is staying temporarily at the Kobe Emigrant Education Centre. It also says that the sender will be departing on 19 December on the ship pictured on the postcard. *Postmarked 10 December, year unknown. Publisher: Kobe Emigrant Education Centre. Accession no.: B32413808G_0008*

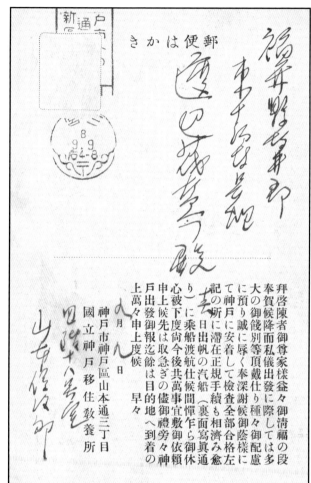

PC6

Featuring the *Montevideo-maru*, also part of O.S.K. Lines (Osaka Shōsen Kaisha) shipping fleet, this postcard indicates the ship's route along with its stopover date in Singapore on the 12th day after departure. A message is pre-printed on the back of the postcard (see page 35 for translation).
Postmarked 9 September, year unknown.
Publisher: Kobe Emigrant Education Centre.
Accession no.: B32413808G_0009

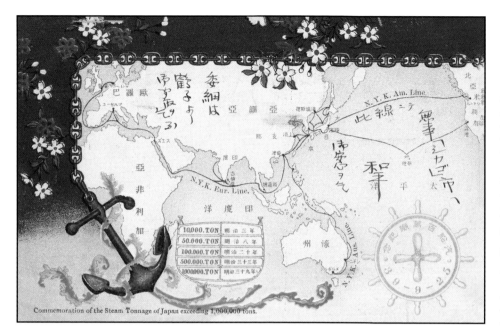

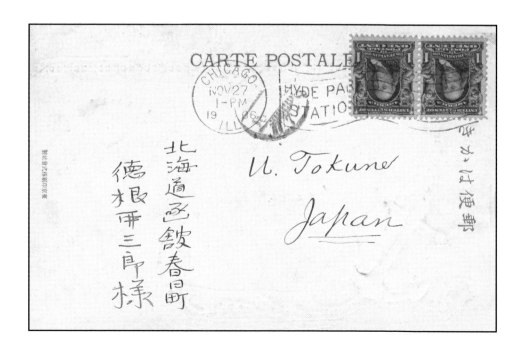

PC7
This postcard was produced to commemorate Nippon Yūsen Kaisha's (NYK) tonnage exceeding 1 million tonnes on 25 September 1906 (Meiji 39th year). The red lines mark out NYK's European and Australian routes, which passed through Singapore. Here, Singapore is indicated in Japanese *kanji* characters "新嘉坡".
Postmarked 27 November 1906. Publisher: Tokyo Publishing Company. Accession no.: B32413808G_0002

routes that spanned vast distances (PC7), reaching beyond the immediate region to faraway destinations such as London and Rio de Janeiro.

On PC8, the international and domestic routes that Nippon Yūsen operated are listed along with the names of major ports of call, such as Colombo and Cape Town. This postcard, postmarked 1906, reflects the demand for travel to these places.

These illustrations of shipping routes were intended not only for Japanese passengers, but for other international travellers as well. Postcards such as PC9 were published in English for Nippon Yūsen's English-speaking passengers.

Postcards were often used by ship passengers to communicate and reassure their loved ones back home that all was well on their travels. Interestingly, some postcards included pre-printed messages with blanks for passengers to fill in with their names and details of their voyage. Such postcards were a boon for semi-literate passengers, who could send word home as they sailed across the seas. On PC8, the pre-printed message on the front of the postcard reads:

> Mr/Ms [blank for passenger's name] conveys his/her regards and wishes to inform you that they have boarded this company's ship, the [blank for ship's name], which set sail on [blank for date] for [blank of destination]. Meiji [blank for year], [blank for month], [blank for date].

The sender of PC8 was headed for Colombo, a journey estimated to take about 18 days (according to the schedules presented on PC5 and PC6). Upon receiving the postcard, the family back home would have been able to trace the ship's route and track roughly where it was in the world.

Migration from Japan

Apart from passengers travelling for business or leisure, there was another group of travellers – Japanese economic migrants. The Japanese government regarded migration as a means of managing its growing population and alleviating the pressures that the Japanese economy was facing. These migrants made their way across the seas to destinations such as the United States, Canada, Europe and Brazil, which, for instance, had attracted Japanese emigrants since 1907 due to demand for cheap labour to work on its coffee plantations.

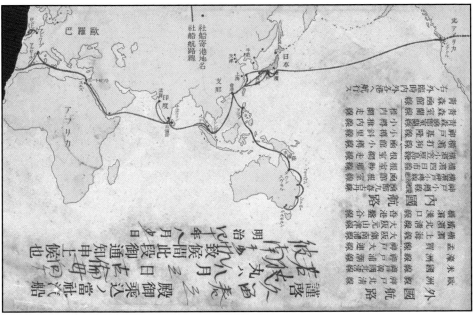

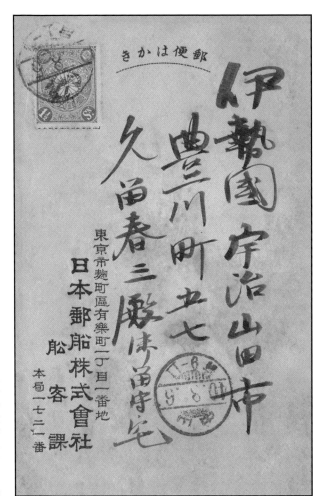

PC8
This postcard maps out the domestic and international
routes of the Nippon Yūsen Kaisha (NYK), with its
European and Australian routes including a stopover
in Singapore. The various ports are indicated on the
right side of the postcard, with a pre-set message at
the bottom for passengers to fill in. The reverse of the
postcard bears the address of the recipient, who lived in
Ujiyamada City and was headed for Colombo.
Postmarked 5 August 1906.
Publisher: Nippon Yūsen Kaisha, Passengers Division.
Accession no.: B32413808G_0004

PC9
Featuring the routes of the Nippon Yūsen Kaisha (NYK) steamers and connecting railway lines, this postcard was sold at NYK ticket offices. It was published in English for its international passengers. The world map indicates that the Japanese national shipping line had a fleet covering international routes. The message on the postcard states that the passenger, Mr Kimijima, had arrived in Port Said, Egypt, on 1 June 1924.
Postmarked 2 June 1924. Publisher: Daie Printing. Accession no.: B32413808G_0013

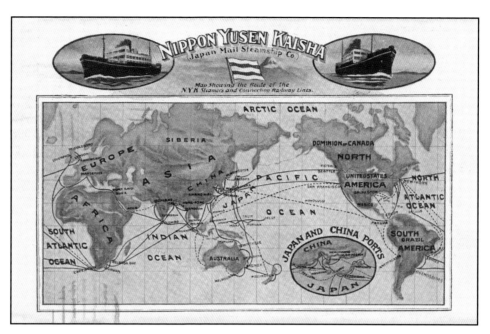

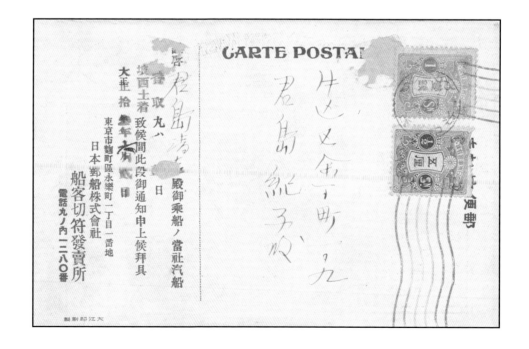

Shipping routes to Europe and Brazil often included stopovers in Singapore from where travellers could send a postcard home.

As seen on the schedule on PC5, Japanese migrants travelling to Brazil via Singapore would set off from the port at Kobe in western Japan, arriving in Hong Kong on the fifth day, Saigon (Ho Chi Minh City) in Vietnam on the ninth, Singapore on the 12th, Colombo in Ceylon (Sri Lanka) on the 18th, Durban and Cape Town in South Africa on the 30th and 34th days respectively, and Rio de Janeiro and Santos in Brazil on the 45th and 46th days. Such postcards highlight Singapore's role as a key port of call along global migration routes.

As part of efforts to promote migration on a large scale, the National Kobe Emigrant Camp (later renamed the Kobe Emigrant Education Centre in 1932) was opened in March 1928, some 20 years after the first group of Japanese emigrants had set sail to Brazil on the *Kasato Maru*. The centre provided temporary free housing to prospective Japanese emigrants from all over Japan for a short period (under 10 days), until they had fulfilled pre-emigration requirements (including attending talks and receiving various vaccinations). The centre continued to run well after the end of the Second World War, and only ceased operations on 31 May 1971.[1]

PC5 and PC6 offer a look into a little-known aspect of these emigration preparations – the provision of postcards by the Kobe Emigrant Education Centre for prospective emigrants to send to loved ones.

These two particular postcards, PC5 and PC6, were sent to Ishikawa Prefecture and Fukui Prefecture, respectively, along the coast of the Sea of Japan, highlighting the various places that prospective emigrants came from. In addition, the need for pre-printed messages on the postcards suggests a low level of literacy among some groups of Japanese emigrants. The printed message on PC6 reads:

> I give my regards to all of you and wish you great happiness. I am deeply grateful to all of you for setting aside money for me and for all your concern. Thanks to all for your [help], I have safely arrived in Kobe and have passed all the [health] examinations. At the address on the left, I have also completed all the proper procedures for my short stint and soon I will board the ship setting sail on [blank for date] (ship is as pictured on the back of this postcard). As I will be setting sail, please permit me to say that I am well and that I wish you all well

in all matters. As things from now will be in haste, this is but a note to let you know that I am setting off from Kobe, and I will write to you of many things once I arrive.

Dated [blank for month] [blank for date]. Kobe City, Kobe District, Yamamoto Dōri San-chōme, Kobe Emigrant Education Centre.[2]

Naval Cooperation and Diplomacy

Singapore was not only a key stop for ships bearing Japanese emigrants to new lands like Brazil, it was also an important port of call for training voyages organised by the Imperial Japanese Navy. These missions were intended to hone the technical skills of rookie cadets by exposing them to conditions on the Pacific Ocean, as well as to raise the public's awareness of the *Nanyō* (South Seas).[3] Even after the abrogation of the Anglo-Japanese Alliance in 1923, Japanese naval ships continued to stop over in Singapore (PC10).[4]

The striking colours and designs on PC11–12 are examples of some common images of the *Nanyō* that the Imperial Japanese Navy used in their postcards. PC12

PC10
This is the official postcard produced for the voyage of the Imperial Japanese Naval Officer Cadets (Taisho 15th year, i.e. 1926), which features their training route. Every academic year, the Imperial Japanese Navy Academy would publish a photo album and postcard in commemoration of their voyage. The two battleships used in this training exercise were the *Izumo* and *Yakumo* and were scheduled to visit Singapore from 24 to 28 July 1926. Postcards like this also helped to create awareness among the Japanese of the South Seas region. *Publisher unknown. Accession no.: B32413808G_0014*

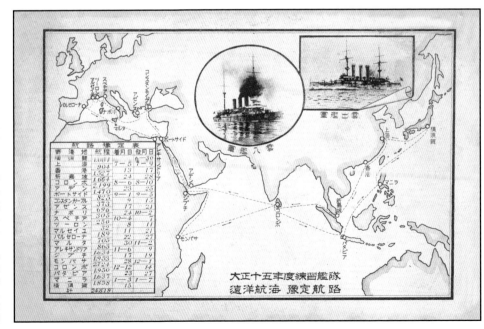

has a particularly interesting presentation that incorporates a tropical sunset and two coconut trees set within a frame. The motif of the coconut tree was frequently used to evoke the exotic South Seas after the Japanese colonisation of Taiwan in 1895.[5] Postcards thus played a role in furthering the Imperial Japanese Navy's aim of depicting the *Nanyō* as an object of consumption and desire and, by extension, to justify colonial ambitions.

Training voyages undertaken by the Imperial Japanese Navy signalled Japan's increasing awareness of political currents beyond its borders. In 1921, Crown Prince Hirohito (later Emperor Hirohito of the Showa era) was the first crown prince in

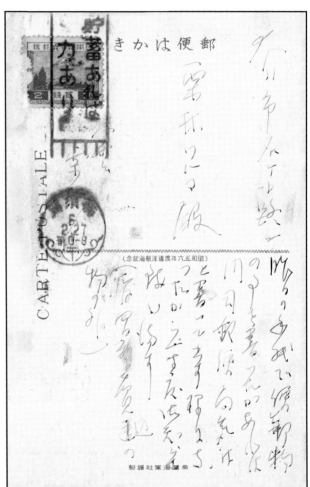

PC11

This postcard was produced for the Voyage of the Imperial Japanese Naval Officer Cadet (Showa 5th and 6th years, i.e., 1930-1931) and features the training route to Marseille, France, led by Vice-Admiral Sakonji Seizō. The two battleships, the *Izumo* and *Yakumo*, were scheduled to be in Singapore from 27 to 31 March 1931. During his time in Singapore, Vice-Admiral Sakonji met with leading members of the Japanese community. Sent domestically from Yokosuka to another address in Japan, this postcard makes mention of how to treat postal matters.
Postmarked 27 February 1931 (before departure from Yokosuka Naval Base).
Publisher: Showa 5th and 6th years' Naval Officer Cadet Training Squadron.
Printer: Japanese Imperial Navy Printing Company.
Accession no.: B32413808G_0016

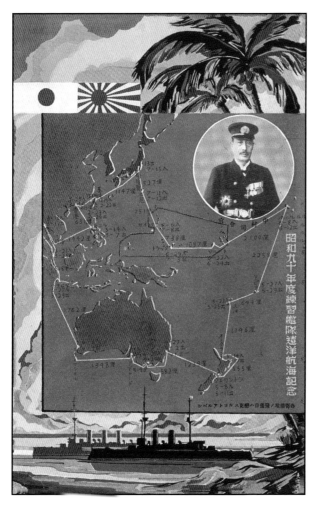

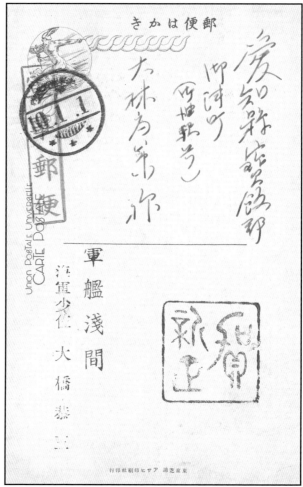

PC12

Posted from the warship *Asama*, this postcard was a military postcard and did not require a postage stamp. It was produced in commemoration of the naval training fleet's overseas voyage from 1934-5 and included Singapore as a stopover. The reverse bears a new year rubber stamp imprint and was sent by Major Ōhashi Kyōzō to an address in Aichi Prefecture.

Postmarked 1 January 1935. Printed by Tokyo Shibaura Asahi Printing Company. Accession no.: B32413808G_0026

Japan's history to embark on a six-month voyage to Britain. Along the way, he stopped at various colonies of the British Empire such as Hong Kong, Singapore and Colombo. This trip was an important and educational one for the Crown Prince as it would equip him for his role as the monarch of a modern empire.[6]

Journalists and photographers in Japan obtained permission to photograph the Crown Prince during his voyage, and these pictures swiftly made their way back home into newspapers and on postcards sold as collectables.[7] PC13 is a classic example: the postcard sets Crown Prince Hirohito's portrait within a laurel wreath against a background of the route he had taken. This postcard was released in commemoration of his return to Japan in 1921; the inclusion of a map, instead of pictures of the event, meant that Japanese subjects could track the route that Hirohito took and trace the path of diplomacy that Japan had carved for itself in the wake of a new world order wrought from the ashes of the First World War.

Conquest

By late 1941, Japan's gruelling war in Northeast Asia and the ongoing war in Europe had spilled over to Southeast Asia. On 7 December 1941, the Pacific War broke out with the bombing of Pearl Harbor on the American territory of Hawaii. Shortly after, Singapore, Britain's "Gibraltar of the East", capitulated to Japanese troops on 15 February 1942. The capture of this strategically and symbolically important bastion of British power in the Far East was celebrated in Japan during the first months of Japan's offensive.

To commemorate this event, the Imperial Japanese Post issued collectable postcards, pictorial postmarks and postage stamps (PC14–16). These commemorative postcards featured Japanese flags emblazoned on locations that had fallen under Japanese control, and often included a geographical representation of Japan in relation to its conquered territories.

PC14 indicates the distances between Japan and these territories, which was likely intended to instil in the Japanese public a sense of national pride in the Imperial Japanese Navy and Imperial Japanese Army's achievements as well as the country's expanding empire. These postcards also capture the heightened sense of euphoria over Japan's resounding success in its military campaign in Southeast Asia.

PC13

This collectable postcard commemorates Crown Prince Hirohito's voyage from Yokohama to Europe with the Third Squadron of the Japanese Imperial Navy. The squadron stopped over in Singapore from 8 to 20 March 1921. The prince's image is presented within the chrysanthemum and laurel wreath (typically Japanese and European motifs), and the flagship and battleship of the fleet are featured on the 3-cent stamp on the reverse of the postcard. The red stamp on the back of the postcard was produced in commemoration of the prince's completion of the voyage and return to Tokyo Palace on 3 September 1921. (The official voyage map is available in the Lim Shao Bin Collection at the National Library. Call no.: RRARE 914.0451 KOT). *Dated 1921. Printed by Insatsu Chōyōkai (under Japan's National Printing Bureau). Accession no.: B32413808G_0011*

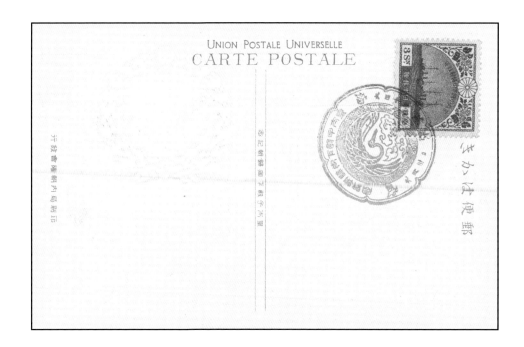

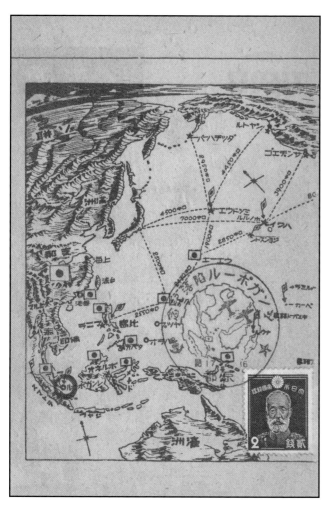

PC14
The postmark stamped on the front of the postcard was produced to mark the fall of Singapore. The Japanese flags on the map indicate locations that had fallen under Japanese control. The postmark, stamped in Kyoto, indicates 16 February 1942, the day after the fall of Singapore.
Postmarked 16 February 1942. Publisher unknown.
Accession no.: B32413808G_0027

PC15
Likely part of a set of postcards produced to mark the fall of Singapore, this postcard features a postmark (stamped in Kobe) that indicates it was issued on 18 February 1942. The red and green postage stamps were also issued to commemorate Japanese victory over Singapore. The red stamp features Nogi Maresuke, a general in the Imperial Japanese Army, and the green one shows Tōgō Heihachirō, admiral of the fleet in the Imperial Japanese Navy. *Postmarked 18 February 1942. Publisher unknown. Accession no.: B32413808G_0028*

PC16
This postcard depicting a world map features three different commemorative postmarks and postage stamps commemorating the fall of Singapore. A Japanese stamp collector had intentionally visited the Post Office on three separate occasions to collect these commemorative postmarks. Reproduced below are: (left) The First Anniversary of the Pacific War (dated 8 December 1942); (middle) The fall of Singapore (dated 20 February 1942); (right) The Second Anniversary of the Pacific War (dated 8 December 1943). *Dated 1942 and 1943. Publisher unknown. Accession no.: B32413808G_0030*

Notes

1   National Diet Library, Japan. 国立神戸移民収容所（神戸移住センター）[Kokuritsu Kobe Imin Shūyōjo (Kōbe Ijyū Sentā-)]. ブラジル移民の100年 [Burajiru Imin no 100 Nen]. Retrieved from National Diet Library.

2   PC5 reads similarly, with slight differences in phrasing.

3   Schencking, J.C. (1999). "The Imperial Japanese Navy and the constructed consciousness of a South Seas destiny, 1872-1921", in *Modern Asian Studies*, 33(4). London: Cambridge University Press, pp. 772–73. (Not available in NLB holdings)

4   Nish, I. H. (1972). *Alliance in Decline: A Study in Anglo-Japanese Relations 1908–23.* London: The Athlone Press. (Call no.: R 327.42052 NIS).

5   Yao, T.S. (2007). ""Images of Taiwan" as visual symbols in official propaganda media during the Japanese colonial period", in デザイン学研究 [*Dezaingakukenkyū* (Journal of the Science of Design)]. 54(1), pp. 59–68. Japanese Society for the Science of Design, p. 63. (Not available in NLB holdings)

6   学習院大学資料館 [Gakushūin daigaku shiryōkan]. (2012). 絵葉書で読み解く大正時代 [Ehagaki de yomitoku Taishō jidai]. Tokyo: Sairyūsha, p. 87. (Not available in NLB holdings)

7   Gakushūin daigaku shiryōkan, 2012, p. 87.

CARTE POSTALE

社會式株船郵船水郵日

きかは便郵

SUPPLEMENTARY POSTCARDS

Nippon Yusen Kaisha S.S. "FUSHIMI MARU."

PC17
Featured on this postcard is the
vessel *Fushimi Maru* belonging
to Nippon Yūsen Kaisha.
*Date unknown. Publisher:
Kobe Mitsumura Insatsu
Bushiki Kaisha. Accession no.:*
B32413808G_0005

PC18
This postcard was produced in commemoration of Crown Prince Hirohito's voyage from Yokohama to Europe, onboard the flagship *Katori* (also shown on the 3-cent stamp). The red stamp on the postcard's reverse side is a commemorative postmark marking the prince's completion of the journey and return to Tokyo Palace on 3 September 1921. The image on the top right of the postcard was the Crown Prince's residence in Akasaka, Tokyo. *Dated 1921. Printed by Choyokai (under Japan's National Printing Bureau). Accession no.: B32413808G_0012*

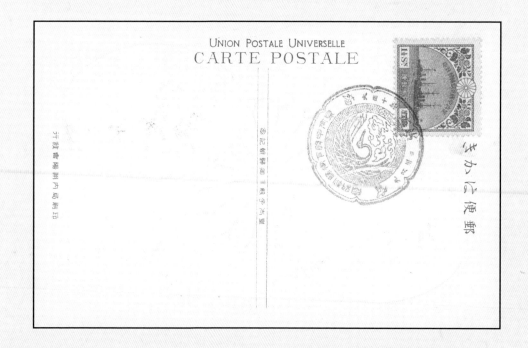

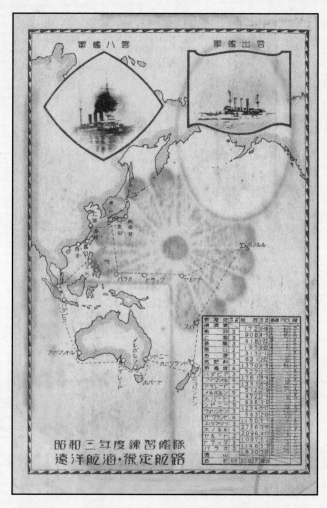

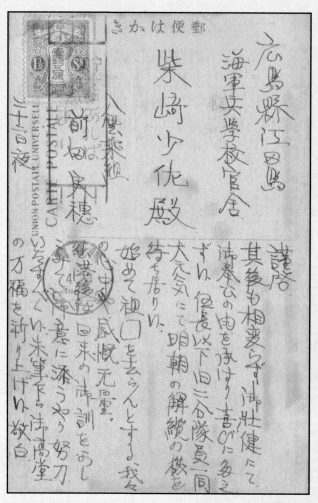

PC19
Dated on the night of 22 April 1928, this postcard was sent by Maeda
Mitsuo, a crew member on board the cruiser *Yakumo*, to Lieutenant
Commander Shibazaki at the official residence of the Imperial Japanese
Naval Academy located on Edajima Island, Hiroshima Prefecture. Maeda
wrote that the crew, while overwhelmed at the thought of leaving Japan,
were in high spirits and looking forward to sailing off the next morning.
The schedule on the front of the card indicates that the ship was to arrive
in Singapore on 28 May. The postcard was postmarked at Yokosuka.
Dated 22 April 1928. Publisher unknown. Accession no.: B32440324K_0051

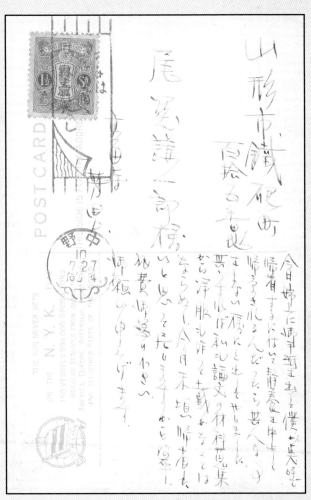

PC20
This postcard features the
S.S. *Fushimi Maru*, which had a
carrying capacity of 11,000 tonnes.
Addressed to an individual living
in Yamagata City, the writer
updates his family of his plans
when he returns home.
Postmarked 27 July 1921.
Publisher unknown.
Accession no.: B32413805D_0086

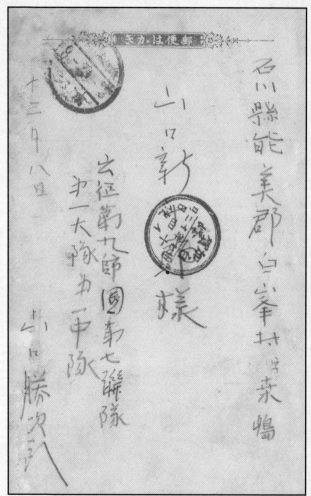

PC21
This postcard of a world map also features
Singapore. This postcard was sent by
Yamaguchi Katsujirō, from Ishikawa
Prefecture, who had been recruited to
serve the Ninth Division (headquartered
at Kanazawa). In his message on the front
of the postcard, he informs the postcard's
recipient(s) of his safe arrival.
Dated December 1918. Publisher unknown.
Accession no.: B32413808G_0007

PC22
The map on this postcard shows the movement between the centres of exchange and trade. The text in red reads: "A million years ago, self-sustaining agriculture arose in Egypt's Memphis, Iran's Susa, and Anau; 6,000 years ago, it became the age of metals and with the use of mules and rafts, there came a time in civilisation of exchange and trade. That centre moved from the city of Uru, then further west and it has now moved to Japan. Nevertheless, we should bear in mind that old centres of exchange and trade were sure to decline after developing."
Date unknown. Publisher: Imperial Flight Association.
Accession no.: B32413808G_0019

PC23
This postcard features the vessel M.S. *Santos Maru*. The red line traces the shipping routes and ports of call. The use of English suggests that the postcard was targeted at an international audience.
Date unknown. Printed and published by a colour printing company in Osaka. Accession no.: B32413808G_0024

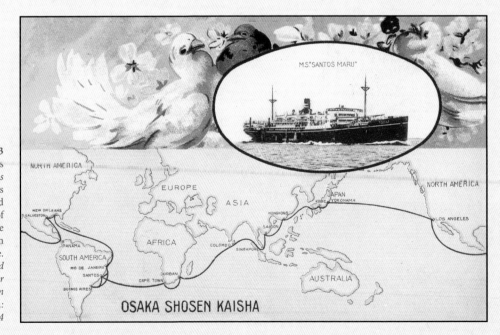

PC24
This map highlights the *Panama-maru*'s regular shipping routes to the South Pacific. Singapore on the map is indicated in *katakana* script.
Date unknown. Publisher: Osaka Shōsen Kaisha. Printed by a colour printing company in Osaka. Accession no.: B32413808G_0020

PC25
This postcard features the main shipping routes to the South Pacific undertaken by the vessel *Kishu Maru*. Singapore is indicated as a port of call on the left of the map.
Date unknown. Publisher: Osaka Shōsen Kaisha. Printed by a colour printing company in Osaka. Accession no.: B32413808G_0021

PC26
Showcased here is
M.S. *La Plata Maru* (referring to
the River Plate on the border of
Argentina and Uruguay), with
images of the various ports of
call en route to South America.
Singapore is featured on
the top left of the postcard.
*Date unknown. Publisher: Osaka
Shōsen Kaisha. Accession no.:
B32413808G_0023*

PC27
This postcard features the battleship
Sōya as it followed the flagship
Aso of the Imperial Japanese Naval
Training Squadron when it stopped
over in Singapore from 16–20 May
1915. Featured within the circle is
the Equatorial Festival, a ritual held
to pray for safe passage whenever a
ship crossed the equator. Its origins
are thought to be from a time when
sailors would pray to the spirits of the
sea for smooth passage through a belt
of windless waters around the equator
called the Inter-tropical Convergence
Zone (known colloquially as "the
doldrums"). This postcard was
printed by the naval magazine *Navy*
in commemoration of the safe return
and completion of the voyage.
*Date unknown. Printed by
Navy magazine. Accession no.:
B32413808G_0025*

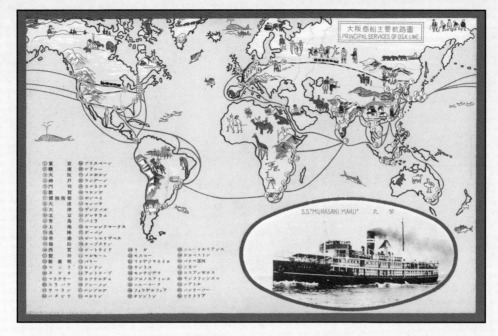

PC28
Showcased here are the principal services of the Osaka Shōsen Kaisha Line, with an insert image of the S. S. *Murasaki Maru*. Singapore, written in Japanese *kanji* characters "新嘉坡", is indicated as the 18th port of call.
Date unknown. Publisher: Osaka Shōsen Kaisha. Printed in Osaka. Accession no.: B32413808G_0022

PC29
This postcard, featuring a globe with text in English, situates Japan as the focus of international communications.
Date unknown. Publisher: Imperial Government Railways of Japan. Printed in Toyko. Accession no.: B32413808G_0032

POSTALE

lina Postale - Post Card

ОЕ ПИСЬМО

CHAPTER 2

EARLY JAPANESE TOURISM IN SINGAPORE

As Singapore was an important port along major international shipping routes, a significant number of Japanese visitors made stopovers in Singapore en route to other destinations on passenger services run by Japanese shipping companies. One such company was Nippon Yūsen Kaisha (mentioned in the previous chapter), which ran a fortnightly service (between May 1898 and November 1939), as well as a monthly one to Europe (between March 1896 and April 1898).[1]

Early Japanese tourists only had a few reliable sources to turn to for travel information: through word-of-mouth from family and friends, published writings by other travellers (such as guidebooks) and, of course, postcards sent by acquaintances who had gone on similar journeys. The postcards in this chapter reveal the impressions that early Japanese travellers had of Singapore, impressions that were in turn relayed to friends and family in Japan, thus shaping the imaginings of the island for those back home.

The information conveyed in the text and pictures of these postcards is very similar to what modern travellers would be interested in today, such as places to visit, sights to see and foods to savour. These postcards offer a glimpse of what Japanese tourists considered quintessential to the experience of visiting Singapore.

Visitors in the early 1900s had only two main transport options available to them – horse-drawn carriages or rickshaws (seen on PC30).[2] Reservations-only private taxi services were only introduced in 1910, so the earliest visitors to Singapore generally relied on *fune heiei* ("ship guards" – Japanese-speaking Malays hired by hotels and inns to distribute flyers and provide tourist information)[3] to flag down transport for them.[4]

To help Japanese tourists find their way around, Japanese-language guidebooks have been produced in Singapore, mostly since the early 1920s. One of the earliest known is *Harada's Guide* published in 1919 by Johdai Printing Works, located at Bras Basah Road. In response to growing requests for more information on Singapore, the Japanese Club (Nihonjin Kurabu) produced the Japanese-language guidebook, *Sekidō wo aruku* (Walking the Equator) in 1939. This guidebook offered useful travel tips, including ways to get around the island (see table below).[6]

GETTING AROUND SINGAPORE

In their advice to Japanese tourists visiting Singapore, the editors of *Sekidō wo aruku* (Walking the Equator) recommended hiring a taxi to get to the heart of the city. From the ship, visitors could place a call for a taxi with any of the taxi companies. The three main Japanese taxi companies operating at the time were Hanaya Cars, Beppu Cars and Nakahara Cars. The editors recommended hiring taxis from Japanese-run companies over non-Japanese ones, not only for ease of communication, but also because of the cheaper rates (prices indicated below in Straits dollars) offered by the former.

	Japanese taxi companies (est.)	Non-Japanese taxi companies (est.)
1st *ri* (3.93 km)	20 cents	50 cents
Per *ri* after 1st *ri*	20 cents	25 cents
1st hour	2 dollars	3 dollars
After 1st hour	Subject to negotiation	75 cents for every 15 minutes

Extracted from Shingapōru Nihonjin Kurabu. (1939). *Sekidō wo aruku* [Walking the Equator]. Tokyo: Dainihon Insatsu Busshi Kaisha, p. 172. (Not available in NLB holdings)

Hotels Where Japanese Stayed

The postcards in this collection offer rare glimpses of the hotels run by Japanese proprietors, which are no longer in existence today and have since faded from

PC30
Scenes such as this gave recipients an idea of what Singapore was like. Addressed to Mr J. Takeda in Tokyo, this postcard features the Central Police Station on South Bridge Road in Singapore (top left) as well as the vessel S.S. *Sanuki Maru* of the NYK (bottom right). The writer says that he has arrived in Singapore and is awaiting his ship to Java. He also notes the temperature on board the ship (86–88°F) and in Singapore (86°F). *Postmarked 22 October 1907. Publisher: Nippon Yūsen Kaisha. Accession no.: B32413805D_0093*

PC31
This postcard features
(clockwise from top left)
the beach along Connaught
Drive, Sekidenkan Hotel
at Beach Road, and the
Botanic Gardens. It was
sent to Tokyo from Tanjong
Pagar in Singapore. This
postcard was sent by an
official from the Ministry
of Agriculture to Yeikichi
Takeda at the Ministry of
Finance, noting that he
would arrive in Singapore
on 17 April.
Postmarked 25 April 1911.
Publisher: Togo & Co.,
Singapore. Accession no.:
B32413805D_0065

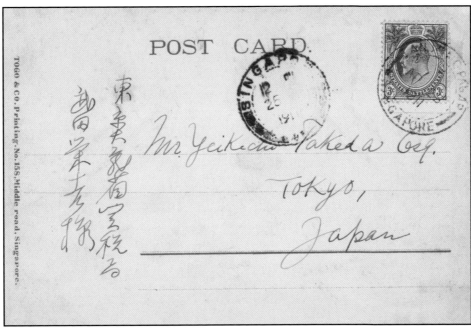

popular memory. One of these was Sekidenkan Hotel (seen on PC31), at Beach Road.[7] The establishment began operations in 1901 and was one of the earliest Japanese hotels in Singapore.[8] Koyokan in Tanjong Katong (PC32) was another such hotel.[9]

Other hotels that were operating in 1939 include Planter's Hotel (PC33) at No. 233 Bencoolen Street, Miyako Hotel (PC34) at No. 15 Beach Road, Toyo Hotel at No. 208 Queen Street, Showa Hotel at No. 25 Bencoolen Street and Sakura Hotel at No. 45 Sophia Road, which offered accommodation packages with daily breakfast from two Straits dollars a night.[10]

Japanese-run hotels and inns were not the only places where Japanese tourists stayed. Japanese travellers seemed to favour Hotel de l'Europe over Raffles Hotel (PC68), which began operations in 1887, as Raffles Hotel was deemed as the luxurious "stronghold of Europeans".[11] Hotel de l'Europe operated from 1857 to 1932 and counted Mori Rintarō (better known as Mori Ōgai, one of the foremost authors of the Meiji period together with Natsume Sōseki), among its notable guests.[12] The hotel also provided postcards to its guests (see PC2 in the Introduction), which cleverly doubled up as advertisements to prospective travellers to Singapore. Toyokan (Toyo Hotel) similarly produced a set of 19 postcards that it distributed to its guests (see page 63).

PC32
Koyokan was a Japanese hotel which was at one time located at the seaside in Tanjong Katong. *Date and publisher unknown. Accession no.: B32413807F_0096*

PC33
Planter's Hotel was located
at 233 Bencoolen Street.
This postcard was sent as a
nengajō, or New Year's card, in
December 1920. It was
sent from Singapore on
31 December 1920 to Taiping
(4 January 1921) and returned
undelivered to Kuala Lumpur
on 5 January 1921.
*Postmarked 31 December 1920.
Publisher unknown. Accession
no.: B32413805D_0089*

PC34
Beach Road was once home
to a string of Japanese hotels
such as Miyako Hotel,
Sekidenkan Hotel, Harima
Hotel, Nippon Hotel
and Navy Hotel.
*Date and publisher
unknown. Accession no.:
B32413806E_0020*

PC35
Tokiwa Garden was
a Japanese *sukiyaki*
establishment located at
17-2 East Coast Road,
Katong. In the 7 March 1933
edition of *The Straits Times*,
it was advertised as serving
"all kinds of refreshments ...
in beautiful surroundings
facing [the] sea".
*Date and publisher
unknown. Accession no.:
B29626253B_0048*

SET OF POSTCARDS DISTRIBUTED
BY TOYOKAN TO HOTEL GUESTS

The proprietor of Toyokan (Toyo Hotel), Ryū Naozaburō, came from Fukuoka to Singapore in 1910 and started the business in 1914. Toyokan distributed postcards to the guests staying with them. Presented here are 10 of the 19 postcards, which can be viewed in larger format from pages 75–80.

Source: Nanyō oyobi nihonjin sha (ed). (1938). *Shingapōru o chūshin ni dōhō katsuyaku – Nanyō no 50 nen*.
Singapore: Nanyō oyobi nihonjin sha, p. 684.

Figure 1

PC36a

PC36b

PC36c

PC36d

PC36e

PC36f

PC36g

PC36j

PC36h

PC36i

Sightseeing

Recurring images featured on postcards include fishing villages on Pulo (Pulau) Brani Island (see PC37 and PC38) off Singapore's southern coast. This was no coincidence given the close proximity of Pulau Brani to Keppel Harbour. The fishing villages on Pulau Brani were very likely the first scenes that greeted travellers when they pulled into Singapore's shores (Figure 2).[13] The sight was a great source of fascination to Japanese travellers, who frequently mentioned it in their written and illustrated accounts of Singapore.[14] Featuring such scenes on postcards was likely a calculated decision to foster perceptions of Singapore as a romantic, tropical destination worthy of a visit, which in turn fuelled the sale of such memorabilia.

Well-known landmarks in Singapore were not the only sights that Japanese travellers encountered as their ships pulled into the harbour. Groups of Malay men rowing up in small boats were a regular sight that greeted a steamship's approach. Those on board larger ships could, for a coin cast into the depths, be treated to a spectacle of local boys and men diving into the water to retrieve the money (Figure 3).[15] Though language barriers would have inhibited conversation, communication nevertheless likely crossed borders through smatterings of fractured English, gesturing and contextual cues.[16] Though this little performance would have amused some, it did not sit well with the consciences of others, who privately lamented the social inequality it represented.[17]

Figure 2
Located close to Keppel Harbour, Pulau Brani was home to fishing villages that were often one of the first sights that greeted travellers as they arrived in Singapore's waters.

Source: Keppel Harbour (New Harbour), 9th ed. (1924). Washington D.C.: Hydrographic Office. From the Lim Shao Bin Collection, National Library, Singapore. Accession no.: B29245117I

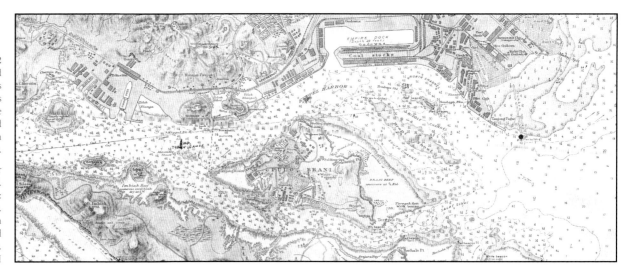

DIVERS AT SINGAPORE.

Figure 3
This 1872 wood engraving by W. B. Sardmerle, titled *Divers at Singapore*, features Malay youths diving into the waters of Keppel Habour to retrieve coins thrown by visitors from their ships. *Courtesy of the National Museum of Singapore, National Heritage Board. Accession no:. 2008-00184*

Singapore. Pulo Brani.

PC37
This scene of a fishing village in the waters off Pulau Brani is one that travellers would have seen as their ships pulled into Singapore's harbour. *Unposted, date unknown. Publisher: Wilson & Co., Singapore. Accession no.: B32413807F_0001*

Singapore. Pulo Brani.

PC38
Another scene of Pulau Brani,
this postcard was addressed
to someone in Russia but
appears not to have been sent.
*Unposted, date unknown.
Publisher: Wilson & Co. for
Hotel de l'Europe & Orchard
Road, Singapore. Accession
no.: B32413807F_0004*

Regardless of such personal misgivings, travellers would have come to expect such scenes in Singapore if they had read the writings of earlier visitors. One such instance can be seen in Mori Ōgai's travel writings on Singapore. His account bears similarities with the observations of Narushima Ryūhoku, a Japanese writer and scholar involved in editing historical annals. Like Narushima, Ōgai wrote of the coin toss, encounters with natives and the red soil of Singapore.[18] In his analysis of Ogai's works, Nishihara Daisuke, surmises that this unconscious yearning to see and experience the same things as earlier travellers stems from the desire to authenticate one's own travel experiences.[19]

Since ships would anchor in Singapore for up to four days, the guidebook *Sekidō wo aruku* (Walking the Equator) included spots for viewing the waxing moon (from the top of "The Gap" on the ridge of South Buona Vista Road) and the waning moon (at Katong beach).

Raffles Square (PC39) was another place of interest as major Japanese companies and banks – such as Nippon Yūsen Kaisha and Bank of Taiwan – and popular department stores such as Robinsons, John Little and Whiteaway Laidlaw were all located here.

The association of certain roads or areas with the local Japanese community may explain why seemingly nondescript places were also depicted on postcards. For instance, located along Serangoon Road were the Japanese Club, Alkaff Gardens (famous for its Japanese-style garden) and the Japanese cemetery, which was the final resting place of the island's long-time Japanese residents, including Futabatei Shimei, a famous Russophile author who died en route to Japan from St Petersburg, Russia.

While most visitors to Singapore made their own plans to tour the island, businessmen and prominent visitors could look forward to personalised tours arranged by the local offices of Japanese firms, such as Mitsui & Co. (also known as Mitsui Bussan or Mitsui Corporation), which opened its Singapore branch in 1891. The company was a major supplier of coal to steamships on the East-West route that bunkered in Singapore. In addition to their regular duties, part of the work of branch managers in Mitsui was to play host to notable Japanese personalities passing through Singapore. These included providing guided tours around the city and arranging accommodation for guests.[20]

PC39
Sent to Tokyo, this postcard features (clockwise from left) Raffles Square, Government House, Katong and North Bridge Road [*sic*: South Bridge Road], which were tourist attractions. This postcard was sent from Singapore on 25 September and arrived in Tokyo via Hong Kong on 13 October 1901. Sent by K. Taguchi to Kezio Taguchi in Tokyo, the writer notes that he is preparing for another departure soon.
Postmarked 13 October 1901. Publisher: G.R. Lambert & Co., Gresham House, Singapore. Accession no.: B32413805D_0031

These acts of hospitality were not done merely out of goodwill; they were an expedient way of cultivating and building relationships with these important travellers, some of whom were powerful political figures, such as Haseba Sumitaka, an influential member in Japan's House of Representatives who visited Singapore in 1906.[21]

Experiences

An entertaining way to soak in the sights of Singapore was to take the electric tram or the omnibus, which plied Middle Road (commonly known as Little Japan).[22] Other recommended activities included shopping and the sampling of local food, as illustrated by the message on PC40:

> […] I tried new food such as watermelon, pineapple, banana, pomelo, and feeling inconvenienced without a watch, bought one from a foreigner for 50 yen, [and] I think this is a steal compared to what you get in Japan […]

The writer might have made his purchases from the temporary stalls that were set up on the decks of Europe-bound ships that pulled into Singapore's harbour. These stalls, operated by enterprising peddlers, sold local souvenirs such as hats, shirts, fans, peacock feathers and ivory chopsticks. More than the exotic range of items available, the most coveted souvenir for Japanese visitors appeared to be the rattan walking stick, a much sought after fashion accessory.[23]

Japanese travellers on transit also enjoyed going on tours to Japanese-owned rubber plantations. Thought to have started sometime between the 1910s and the 1920s, these plantation tours were apparently highly popular.[24] PC41's writer describes the rubber-extraction process demonstrated on such tours: "It's a rubber tree. When you cut the bark, the sap comes out and from that they make rubber."

The leaves and seeds of the rubber trees were regarded as suitable souvenirs, to be given away as specimens, or donated to schools in Japan for educational purposes. To make it easier to carry them back home, rubber seeds were packed into boxes which were then sold for 2 to 3 dollars each.[25]

While rubber plantations were places of curiosity for the ordinary Japanese tourist, they were a matter of great importance to Japanese businessmen who had staked their

The Museum in, Singapore.

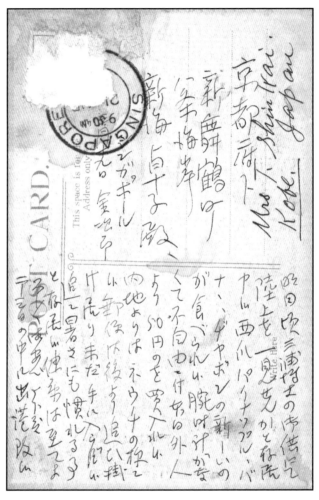

PC40
Featuring the Raffles Museum, this postcard bound for
Kyoto (the English address states "Kobe", but the Japanese
address states "Kyoto"). The writer had accompanied a
Dr Miura and sampled a variety of fruits. He also
marvelled at how inexpensive it was to buy a watch in
Singapore (50 Japanese yen).
Postmarked 21 March, year unknown. Publisher unknown.
Accession no.: B32413805D_0117

investments in the rubber estates, with hopes of striking it rich. Unbeknownst to these Japanese entrepreneurs, their foray into the industry would coincide with the end of the rubber boom after the First World War (1914–18). This meltdown of the industry impacted not only the fortunes of rubber estate owners but also members of the local Japanese community who had invested in the plantations.

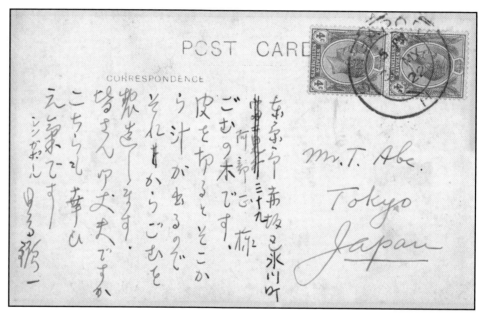

PC41
Addressed to T. Abe in Tokyo, this postcard shows workers at a rubber plantation in Singapore tapping for rubber. The message on the back of this postcard describes the rubber tapping process.
Postmarked 31 May 1922.
Publisher unknown.
Accession no.: B32413805D_0092

DAY TRIP ITINERARIES

Sekidō wo aruku (Walking the Equator) provided recommendations of must-see places in Singapore and offered suggestions on self-guided day trip itineraries that readers could follow, each lasting three to four hours. The postcards mentioned below can be viewed on pages 81–102.

Itinerary (estimated time needed)	Places to see (in order)
This tour focuses on individual buildings and attractions. (3 hours)	Thomas Cook Company → Clifford Pier (PC42, PC43) → Headquarters of the Postal Office (PC44, PC45) → the Nippon Yūsen Kaisha (NYK) → the Bank of Taiwan (PC46, PC47) → department stores such as Robinsons lined up along Raffles Square (PC48) → Anderson Bridge (PC49, PC50) → Victoria Memorial Hall (PC51, PC52) → the Supreme Court → the Cenotaph → the Singapore Cricket Club (PC53, PC54) → St Andrew's Cathedral (PC55, 56) → Raffles Museum (PC57, PC58) → Government House (PC59) → the Botanic Gardens (PC60, PC61, PC62, PC63) → the Japanese shrine → the reservoir (PC64, PC65) and the Island Golf Club → Tan Tock Seng Hospital → the sports grounds of the Japanese Club → the Alkaff Gardens (PC66, PC67) → the Japanese cemetery → Katong Beach → Happy World → Raffles Hotel (PC68)
This tour features scenic driving routes with idyllic village scenes. (3.5–4 hours)	Ship → Keppel Road → Robinson Road → Raffles Square/South Bridge Road → Tanjong Katong Beach (PC69, PC70, PC71) → East Coast Road → Tanah Merah (Budo Village) → Geylang Road (PC72) → Paya Lebar village → Serangoon Road (through the rubber plantations) → Punggol coastline (for the only zoo in Singapore) → Japanese cemetery → Ship
This tour incorporates a trip to Johor. (4 hours)	Chinatown → Japanese Primary School → Japanese Association → Travellers' Palms near the pond of the Government House → the red bridge at Thomson Road → Johor (Sultan's Palace, the city hall, mosques)

Adapted from Shingapōru Nihonjin Kurabu. (1939). *Sekidō wo aruku* [Walking the Equator]. Tokyo: Dainihon Insatsu Busshi Kaisha, pp. 175–179. (Not available in NLB holdings)

Notes

1   Writers' personal correspondence with Satō Yoshifumi, Assistant Director, NYK Maritime Museum.

2   The rate for one horse-drawn carriage was 2 yen 50 sen in 1900. 西原大輔 [Daisuke Nishihara]. (2017). 日本人のシンガポール体験：幕末明治から日本占領下・戦後まで [Nihonjin no Shingapōru Taiken: Bakumatsumeiji kara nihonsenryōka. sengo made]. Kyoto: Jinbun Shoin, p. 55. (Not available in NLB holdings)

3   Nishihara, 2017, p. 56.

4   西村竹四郎 [Takeshirō Nishimura]. (1911). 在南三十五年 [Zainan sanjūgo nen]. Tokyo: Ankyūsha, p. 13. (Not available in NLB holdings); Nishihara, 2017, p. 56.

5   The Japanese Club, established in 1922 by notable Japanese residents in Singapore, was an affiliated organisation of the Japanese Association, Singapore. It was a private social club, and its relatively high monthly membership fees suggest that it catered to individuals with higher socio-economic statuses. The club's activities included hosting speakers for lectures, sponsoring tennis matches and holding flower arrangement exhibitions. The Japanese Association. (2016). シンガポール日本人社会百年史 ： 星月夜の耀 [100 Year History of Japanese Community in Singapore (1915–2015)]. Singapore: The Japanese Association, p. 76. (Call no.: RSING 305.895605957 ONE)

6   シンガポール日本人クラブ [Shingapōru Nihonjin Kurabu]. (1939). 赤道を歩く [Sekidō wo aruku]. Tokyo: Dainihon Insatsu Busshi Kaisha, p. 1. (Not available in NLB holdings)

7   Beach Road was home to a string of Japanese hotels, such as Sekidenkan Hotel (5-8 Beach Road), Miyako Hotel (5-4 Beach Road), Harima Hotel (5-13 Beach Road), Nippon Hotel (5-15 Beach Road) and Navy Hotel (5-15 Beach Road). Many of these hotels later relocated. 佃光治 [Tsukuda Mitsuharu]. (1917). 馬來に於ける邦人活動の現況 [Marai ni okeru hōjin katsudō no genkyō] Singapore: Nanyō oyobi nihonjinsha, p. 273. (Call no.: RRARE 305.89560595 TSU -[LSB]) Digitised book available on BookSG.

8   Shingapōru Nihonjin Kurabu, 1939, p. 10 of advertisements.

9   Untitled. [Microfilm: NL 00510]. (1923, September 19). *The Straits Times*, p. 11.; Koyokan was likely also operating as a brothel – its proprietor was fined in 1922 for allowing his premises to be used for "immoral purposes", i.e., prostitution. See: Lodgings Misused. [Microfilm: NL 1967]. (1922, January 5). *The Singapore Free Press and Mercantile Advertiser (Weekly)*, p. 3.

10   Shingapōru Nihonjin Kurabu, 1939, pp. 8–9 of advertisements. See also 伊藤友治郎 [Tomojiro Itō]. (1914). 南洋群嶋寫真畫帳：附南洋事情 [Nanyō Guntō Shashin Gachō: Fu Nanyō Jijō]. Eiryō Penan Shi: Nanyō chōsakai, p. 22 (Call no.: RRARE 959 ITO) to see a close-up image of the entrance of Miyako Hotel. A black-and-white digital copy is available for viewing on the National Diet Library's website.

11   Nishihara writes that it was deemed as a "*ōbeijin no gajō tarumono kokyū hoteru*". The word "*gajō*" tends to be used when referring to the enemy's stronghold or bastion. Nishihara, 2017, p. 36.

12   Nishihara, 2017, p. 51.

13   Nishihara suggests that Pulau Brani was likely the model for the water villages depicted in the works of 今村紫紅 [Shikō Imamura], 熱国之巻 （朝之巻）[Nekkoku no Maki (Asa no Maki)] [Scrolls of Tropical Countries (Morning Scroll)], which was designated as an important cultural property in Japan, indicating that the sight of Pulau Brani likely constituted one of the key Japanese perspectives of Singapore. Nishihara, 2017, p. 88. A digital copy of the scroll is available for viewing on the National Institutes for Cultural Heritage website.

14 Nishihara, 2017, p. 88.

15 These scenes were not limited to Japanese visitors. Other travellers also recorded similar experiences, see Hoyle, F. (1899). "Impressions of a voyage to China and Japan", in *The Journal of the Manchester Geographical Society* Vol. XV, pp. 212-217. Manchester Geographical Society, Manchester, p. 213. (Not available in NLB holdings)

16 Nishihara cites a source from Torahiko Terada, which records the men shouting, "I say; Herr Meister, far away, far away, one dollar, all dive." Nishihara, 2017, p. 79.

17 Nishihara, 2017, pp. 77–79.

18 Nishihara, 2017, pp. 53–54.

19 Nishihara, 2017, p. 54.

20 Nishihara, 2017, pp. 67–69.

21 Nishihara, 2017, p. 68.

22 Shingapōru Nihonjin Kurabu, 1939, p. 178.

23 Nishihara, 2017, pp. 80–81.

24 Nishihara, 2017, p. 93.

25 Shingapōru Nihonjin Kurabu, 1939, p. 198.

CARTE POSTALE
Postkarte – Cartolina Postale – Post Card
ОТКРЫТОЕ ПИСЬМО

きかっは便郵

MADE IN JAPAN

SUPPLEMENTARY POSTCARDS

Figure 1
The envelope for a set of
19 postcards distributed by
Toyokan to its guests. Ten of
them (PC36a–36j) are presented
in the following pages.
*Date and publisher
unknown. Accession no.:
B32413805D_0172*

TOYO HOTEL,
131, MIDDLE ROAD,
SINGAPORE.

PC36a
The Singapore waterfront was once lined by the (from left to right) Ocean Building, Alkaff Arcade, Union Building, Hong Kong and Shanghai Bank (HSBC) and the Fullerton Building. *Date and publisher unknown. Accession no.: B32413805D_0172*

PC36b
Originally located at the Padang, the statue of Sir Stamford Raffles was moved to a site in front of the Victoria Memorial Hall at Empress Place in 1919. There, the statue was framed by a semi-circular colonnade of the Italian Doric order with a marble-lined pool with fountain jets before it. *Date and publisher unknown. Accession no.: B32413805D_0172*

PC36c
The Fullerton Building, which was officially opened in 1928, was home to the General Post Office. It was gazetted as a national monument on 7 December 2015.
Date and publisher unknown. Accession no.: B32413805D_0172

PC36d
This postcard features Anderson Bridge with the General Post Office in the background.
Date and publisher unknown. Accession no.: B32413805D_0172

PC36e
This postcard features an aerial view of the Singapore waterfront. Visible are the Ocean Building (foreground, right), the tidal basin and the eastern part of Sentosa island in the background. *Date and publisher unknown. Accession no.: B32413805D_0172*

PC36f
Presented here are, from left to right, Union House, Hong Kong and Shanghai Bank (HSBC) and the Fullerton Building. Union House and HSBC were designed by renowned architectural firm Swan and Maclaren. Fullerton Building was designed by Major Percy Hubert Keys and his assistant Frank Dowdeswell. *Date and publisher unknown. Accession no.: B32413805D_0172*

PC36g
A view of Raffles Quay with Ocean Building on the right. There were four Ocean Buildings constructed over the years, the first in 1866 and the present one known as the Ocean Financial Centre completed in 2011. *Date and publisher unknown. Accession no.: B32413805D_0172*

PC36h
This postcard features a rare view of Singapore and was likely taken atop of the Bank of Taiwan, which could probably only be accessed by the Japanese. The building on the right is the former General Post Office, prior to its moving to Fullerton Building. The shoreline in the background is Tanjong Rhu and Katong. *Date and publisher unknown. Accession no.: B32413805D_0172*

PC36i
A scene featuring Malay girls
at a river in Singapore.
*Date and publisher
unknown. Accession no.:
B32413805D_0172*

PC36j
Rubber tappers of Indian descent
working at Ono Plantation, a
Japanese-owned rubber plantation.
While the postcard places the location
as Singapore, Ono Plantation was
actually located in Johor.
*Date and publisher unknown.
Accession no.: B32413805D_0172*

クリッフオード桟橋ト防波堤　（新嘉坡）

PC42

PC42–72 feature locations and landmarks commonly included in day trip itineraries for Japanese visitors to Singapore (see page 72). The Japanese text on top of this postcard reads: "Clifford Pier and breakwater (Singapore)". *Date and publisher unknown. Accession no.: B32440324K_0142*

PC43

This postcard featuring Clifford Pier was sent by Ogawa Tōru to Hashimoto T. in Tokyo, Japan, as a New Year's greeting card. *Postmarked 19 December [193?]. Publisher unknown. Accession no.: B32413805D_0106*

Union Building, Singapore

PC44
While this postcard features
Union Building, it interestingly
also captures Fullerton Building
(extreme right) in the midst
of construction. Work on
Fullerton Building commenced
in 1924 and it officially opened
four years later (PC45 shows the
completed building). This card
was part of a booklet called
12 Views of Singapore.
Date unknown. Publisher:
M.W.P. Singapore.
Accession no.: B34488213K

POST CARD

378936

M. W. P., Singapore.

General-Post-Office, Singapore

PC45
A view of the General Post Office. The sender seems to be an employee of Mitsui & Co. in Kobe. He writes to his colleagues to inform them that he is well and thanks them for their well wishes. He also mentions his frustration at not being able to accomplish what he had hoped to in Singapore as a result of the economic recession.
Postmarked 1 December 1930. Publisher unknown. Accession no.: B32413805D_0105

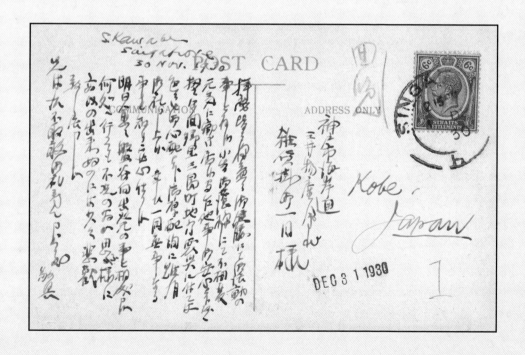

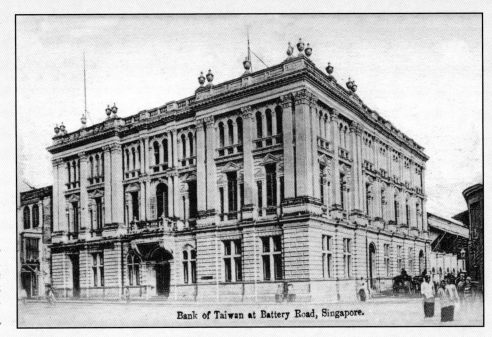

Bank of Taiwan at Battery Road, Singapore.

PC46
Bank of Taiwan located on Battery Road. It was the representative of the Bank of Japan in Southeast Asia. *Date and publisher unknown.* *Accession no.: B32413806E_0007*

Bank of Taiwan at Battery Road. Singapore

PC47
A view of the Bank of Taiwan on Battery Road. *Date and publisher unknown. Accession no.: B32413806E_0009*

商業銀行ト　ラツフルス通リ　（新嘉坡）

PC48
This postcard is captioned "Commercial banks and Raffles Place (Singapore)". This view of Raffles Place faces the Mercantile Bank, flanked by John Little (left) and Robinson & Co. Ltd (right). Raffles Place, once known as Commercial Square, was and still is the heart of Singapore commerce. *Date and publisher unknown. Accession no.: B32440324K_0144*

Anderson Bridge, Singapore.

PC49
Anderson Bridge was officially opened in 1910 by John Anderson, governor of the Straits Settlements, after whom the bridge was named. *Date unknown. Publisher: Yamato & Co. Accession no.: B32440324K_0062*

Anderson Bridge, Singapore.

Victoria Memorial Hall, Singapore.

PC50
This Japanese printed postcard depicts
Anderson Bridge, which was designed by
municipal engineer Robert Pierce and his
assistant D.M. Martin. It comprises three
steel arches, two rusticated arches and
a fluted pier at each end.
Date and publisher unknown.
Accession no.: B32440324K_0063

PC51
This Japanese printed postcard shows
Victoria Memorial Hall. The performance
venue was designed in the popular
Palladian style and was connected to
Victoria Town Hall by a clock tower.
Date and publisher unknown. Accession no.:
B32413805D_0166

H 287   Victoria Memorial Hall, Singapore.

PC52
Bound for Sapporo, this postcard features Victoria Memorial Hall. Writing from Singapore, the sender notes that he had arrived by steamship after 12 days at sea. He also writes about the island's climate. This postcard was printed in Japan. *Postmarked 26 June 1923. Publisher unknown. Accession no.: B32413805D_0099*

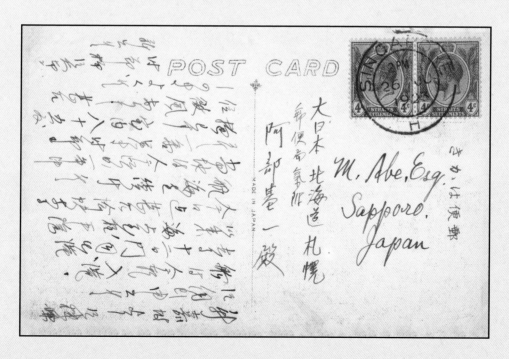

Cricket Club, Singapore.   No. 8

PC53
This Japanese printed postcard shows the Singapore Cricket Club, which was established in 1852 and began life as a wooden-hut pavilion in the 1860s. This image was taken before the construction of the Club's new wings. *Date and publisher unknown. Accession no.: B32413805D_0141*

Singapore Cricket Club, Singapore

PC54
This Japanese postcard features the Singapore Cricket Club on the left and Hotel de l'Europe on the right. The large field in the foreground is the Padang. *Date and publisher unknown. Accession no.: B32440324K_0054*

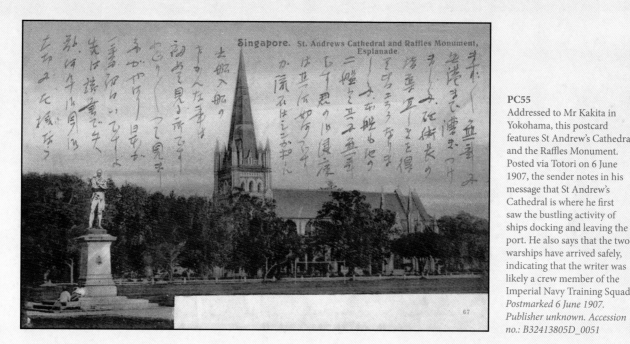

PC55
Addressed to Mr Kakita in
Yokohama, this postcard
features St Andrew's Cathedral
and the Raffles Monument.
Posted via Totori on 6 June
1907, the sender notes in his
message that St Andrew's
Cathedral is where he first
saw the bustling activity of
ships docking and leaving the
port. He also says that the two
warships have arrived safely,
indicating that the writer was
likely a crew member of the
Imperial Navy Training Squad.
*Postmarked 6 June 1907.
Publisher unknown. Accession
no.: B32413805D_0051*

(27)   St. Andrew's Cathedral, Singapore.

Raffles Museum, Singapore.

PC56
This made-in-Japan postcard features
St Andrew's Cathedral, which was built
between 1856 and 1864. The postcard
was sent from the Straits Settlements to
North Wales.
Dated 22 December 1910.
Publisher unknown. Accession no.:
B32413805D_0058

PC57
This Japanese printed postcard
features a view of Raffles Museum
with its iconic 90-foot high dome.
Today, it is the National Museum
of Singapore.
Date and publisher unknown.
Accession no.: B32413805D_0149

(18)   Raffles Museum & Library, Singapore.

PC58
This made-in-Japan
postcard features the Raffles
Museum and Library. The
Raffles Museum and Library
building opened in 1887. In
1960, the library moved into
its own building.
*Date and publisher
unknown. Accession no.:
B32413807F_0010*

Government House, Singapore.

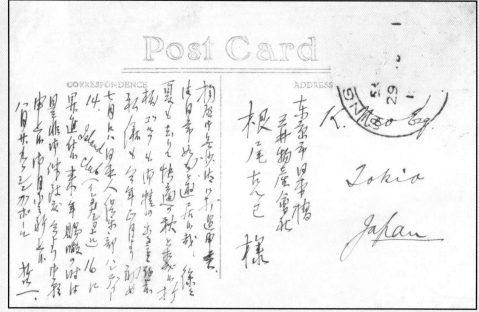

PC59
Addressed to Mr Neo who was working at Mitsui & Co. in Tokyo, Japan, this postcard features Government House (now the Istana) in the background. The message contains details of the sender's experiences in Singapore, noting that his golf handicap was 14 at the Japanese Club, and 16 at the Island Club.
Postmarked 29 August, year unknown.
Publisher unknown. Accession no.:
B32440324K_0036

Singapore. Botanic Garden.

PC60
This postcard featuring the Botanic Gardens was addressed to T. Matsuki in Tokyo. The brief message on the front of the postcard says that the sender is writing from "far away" and that the picture is of Singapore. *Postmarked 15 March 1906 (Singapore); 19 March 1906 (Hong Kong); 24 March 1906 (Tokyo). Publisher unknown. Accession no.: B32440324K_0011*

PC61
In this postcard featuring the Botanic Gardens in Singapore, the sender writes to his acquaintance, Mr Yamada T. residing in Kobe, to express his concern about the "Tokyo earthquake disaster". This likely refers to the 1923 Great Kantō Earthquake, which occurred on 1 September 1923. *Dated 5 November 1923. Publisher unknown. Accession no.: B32440324K_0140*

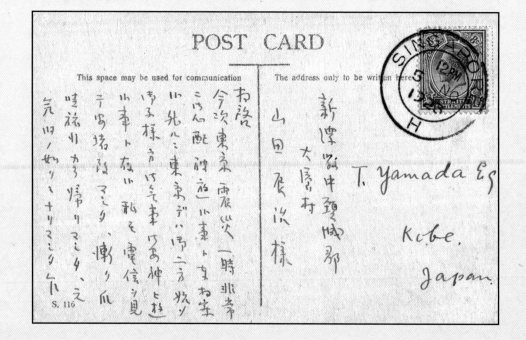

PC62
Also featuring the Botanic Gardens in Singapore, the sender of this postcard writes to a Mrs Takeda in Tokyo, informing her of the writer's arrival in Singapore. The writer also notes that he is staying at Hotel de l'Europe. *Publisher unknown. Accession no.: B32413805D_0055*

PALMS, BOTANICAL GARDENS. SINGAPOER.

POST-CARD.

This Space for Communication   For the Address only.

163 Middle Road Singapore

Mr. E. Takeda

Tokio

Japan

PC63
This postcard, featuring palms at
the Botanic Gardens in Singapore,
was sent as a New Year's greeting
card to Takeda E. at the Ministry of
Finance in Tokyo from Murata at
163 Middle Road, Singapore.
*Dated 1 January 1911 (45th year
of Meiji). Publisher unknown.
Accession no.: B32413805D_0063*

貯 水 池　（新嘉坡）

PC64
The Japanese text at
the upper edge of this
postcard reads: "Reservoir
(Singapore)". Featured here
is MacRitchie Reservoir,
which was a place of
interest for many travellers.
*Date and publisher
unknown. Accession no.:
B32440324K_0147*

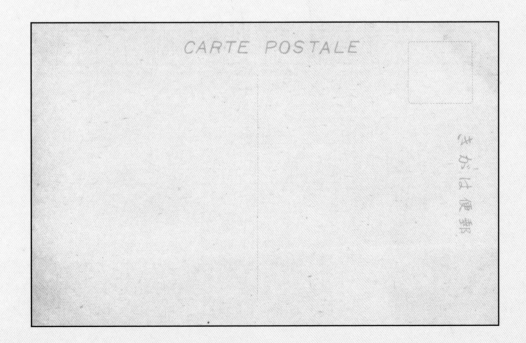

CARTE POSTALE

PC65
This made-in-Japan postcard shows what was known as the Impounding Reservoir at Thomson Road. Constructed in 1867 with funds donated by philanthropist Tan Kim Seng, it was the first reservoir in Singapore. It was later enlarged and named the Thomson Road Reservoir in 1907. It was renamed again as the MacRitchie Reservoir in honour of the municipal engineer, James MacRitchie, who designed and built the reservoir. *Date and publisher unknown. Accession no.: B32413805D_0164*

The Lake is Impounding Reservoir Thomson Road, Singapore.

PC66
Locations with Japanese associations were often featured on postcards, such as Alkaff Gardens which was famous for its Japanese-style garden. *Date and publisher unknown. Accession no.: B32413806E_0001*

Alkaff Garden, Singapore.

Alkaff Garden, Singapore.

PC67
Alkaff Gardens was built in the style of a Japanese garden and was a popular destination for locals and Japanese tourists. The garden also had a Japanese teahouse. The picture on this postcard is also featured in an advertisement for Alkaff Gardens in the 31 May 1930 issue of the *Malayan Saturday Post*. On the far left of the postcard is a *tōrō*, a traditional Japanese lantern made of stone. *Date and publisher unknown. Accession no.: B32413806E_0002*

Singapore, Raffles Hotel.

PC68
Located on Beach Road, Raffles Hotel was a well-known landmark and hotel popular with European travellers. Raffles Hotel was gazetted as a national monument in 1987, and re-gazetted in 1995 with changes to its boundaries. *Date and publisher unknown. Accession no.: B32413807_0009*

Tanjong Katong, Singapore

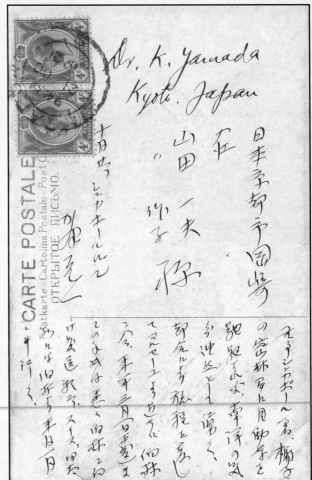

PC69
This postcard is addressed to Mr K. Yamada in Kyoto. In it, the writer muses about the dense growth of coconut trees and how the rushing waves embody the essence of the South Seas. The writer also notes that he will set sail for Berlin on 1 November, and remain there until March 1922.
Postmarked 21 October 1921 (Singapore). Publisher unknown.
Accession no.: B32413805D_0087

Tanjiong Katong and Sea View Hotel, Singapore.   No. 27

Sea View Hotel, Singapore.

PC71
The Sea View Hotel at Tanjong Katong opened
in 1906. It fronted the sea and was surrounded
by a grove of coconut trees. It was described
by *Willis's Singapore Guide* (1936) as one of
Singapore's leading hotels and was reputed to
be a place for guests looking to rest
and recuperate after an illness.
Date and publisher unknown.
Accession no.: B32440324K_0043

PC70
This made-in-Japan postcard features
Tanjong Katong Beach and the Sea
View Hotel.
Dated c.1907–25. Publisher unknown.
Accession no.: B32413805D_0157

PC72
Featured on this postcard is
Gayland (Geylang) Road in
Singapore. The postcard was
addressed to Y. Shimidzu in
Bombay (Mumbai), care of
shipping company
Nippon Yūsen Kaisha.
*Postmarked 17 October 1912
(Singapore). Publisher: Max
H. Hilckes. Accession no.:
B32413805D_0064*

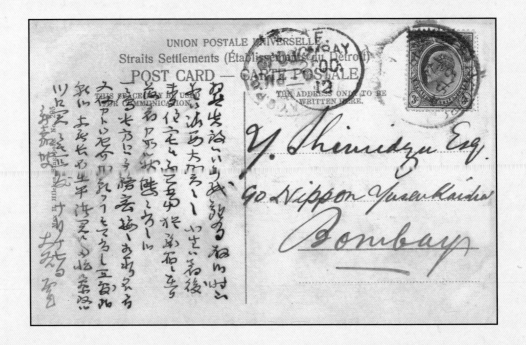

(5) *It is like this all the year* Esplanade, Singapore. *round – left is the sea* *Right side*

PC73
This made-in-Japan postcard features the Esplanade in Singapore. The card does not seem to have been posted as it does not bear a stamp, though it was destined for London. The front of the postcard notes: "It is like this all the year round – left is the sea, right is the Cricket Club." The message on the reverse side reads: "Dear Madge, Many thanks for card[.] glad you are enjoying yourself[.] I'm O.K. as usual, quite alive you know. Kindest regards, Percy." On the right side of the card, the writer has further added: "Love on a post-card would never do" and underlined it. The writer included a small sketch of a rickshaw, a woman holding a parasol and a tree.
Dated November 1910. Publisher unknown. Accession no.: B32413805D_0071

Traveller's Trees, Singapore.

PC74
Featuring a row of Traveller's Trees, this postcard was likely made in Japan as its reverse bears the Japanese words for "postcard". *Date and publisher unknown. Accession no.: B32413805D_0161*

PC75
This postcard features a
scene from Fujiyama in
Japan. It was sent from
Singapore to Paris, France.
Dated November 1906.
Publisher unknown.
Accession no.:
B32413805D_0050

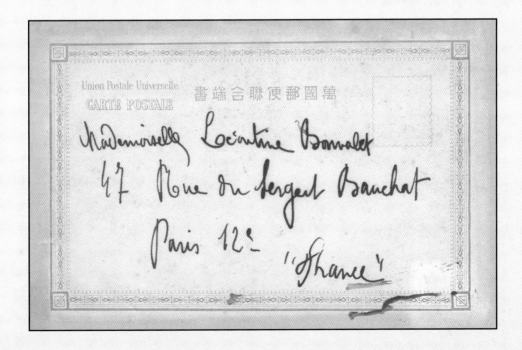

Mt. Fuji from Hakone Lake   望遠士富リヨ湖ノ芦根箱

PC76
Featured on this postcard is a tranquil scene of a small sailing boat on Lake Hakone with Mount Fuji in the background. *Dated June 1915. Publisher unknown. Accession no.: B32413805D_0075*

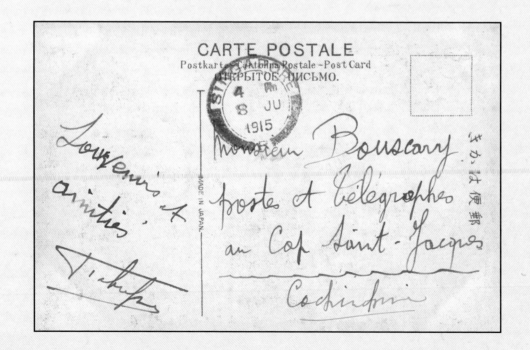

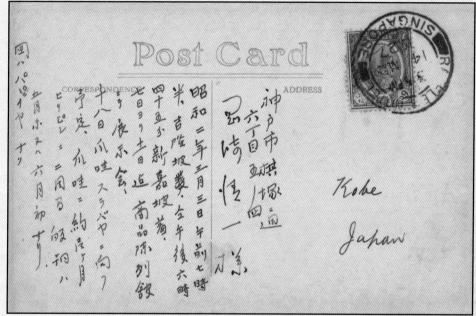

PC77

In this postcard bound for Kobe, the sender updates the addressee of his arrival in Kuala Lumpur and Singapore as well as his travel plans. The writer was in Singapore for a product exhibition held at the Japanese Commercial Museum from 7–11 March 1927, before heading to places such as Surabaya and the Philippines. He also explains that the image on the postcard shows papayas.
Postmarked from Raffles Hotel in Singapore. Dated 1927. Publisher unknown. Accession no.: B32413805D_0104

Traveller's tree, Singapore.   No. 39

CARTE POSTALE
Postkarte - Cartolina Postale - Post Card
ОТКРЫТОЕ ПИСЬМО

MADE IN JAPAN

PC78
Captioned "Traveller's Tree, Singapore", this
postcard was made in Japan. The Traveller's Tree
(*Ravenala madagascariensis*) was known as such
due to the water that would accumulate at the
base of its leaves, which could be slashed open
and used as drinking water in an emergency.
While the tree is native to Madagascar, it is also
cultivated globally.
Date and publisher unknown.
Accession no.: B32413805D_0162

Singapore. Hongkong and Shanghai Bank.

PC79
Addressed to a K. Okubo, this postcard features the Hongkong and Shanghai Bank (HSBC) in Singapore. The sender notes that he is passing through Singapore, where the temperature is 85–86°F and weather reasonably comfortable. While the address in English states "Kobe", the precise location is provided in Japanese as Kanazawa City (Ishikawa Prefecture). This way of writing addresses is still practiced today where the nearest large city is stated in English and the exact address in Japanese. *Postmarked 16 March 1905 (Singapore); 23 March 1905 (Hong Kong); date unknown (Koda); 30 March 1905 (Kobe). Publisher unknown. Accession no.: B32413805D_0045*

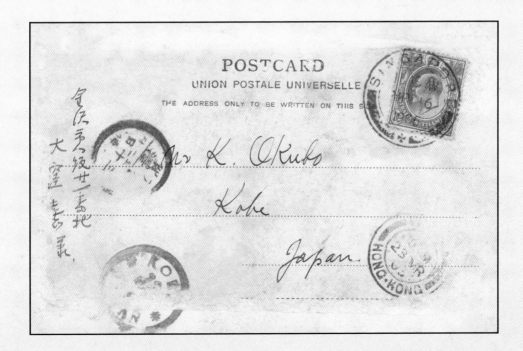

PC80
Addressed to K. Okubo in
Kanazawa City, the writer
of this postcard featuring
a native village notes
that despite Singapore's
proximity to the equator,
it is not too hot.
*Postmarked 9 July 1906
(Singapore); 16 July 1906
(Hong Kong); 25 July 1906
(Kanazawa). Publisher
unknown. Accession no.:
B32413805D_0046*

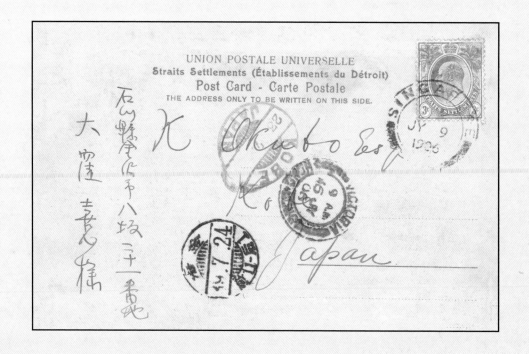

PC81
Here, men and women dressed
in traditional Japanese clothes
are seen with a rickshaw under
a sakura tree. Produced in
Japan, this postcard was sent
from Singapore to Edinburgh,
Scotland with the message
"Am watching for a letter
every day …".
*Dated July 1904. Publisher
Unknown. Accession no.:
B32413805D_0113*

CHAPTER 3

EARLY JAPANESE COMMUNITY IN SINGAPORE

During the 16th and 17th centuries, Japanese traders paved the way for the influx of Japanese migrants to parts of Southeast Asia, such as Vietnam, Thailand, the Philippines, Myanmar and Singapore.[1] In 1932, Nishimura Takeshirō,[2] an important figure in the early Japanese community in Singapore and one of the island's first Japanese doctors, noted in his diary that early emigrants such as himself were like the "foundation stones used in the construction of harbours": they enabled the advancement of Japanese interests overseas but were not recognised for their instrumental roles. Lamenting the lack of acknowledgement of the efforts put in by these pioneers, Nishimura added that if there "came along an individual who might shed […] tears for these foundation stones, they [the foundation stones] might begin shaking out of their excessive happiness."[3]

In this chapter, we look at the lives of early Japanese settlers in Singapore through picture postcards that were addressed to or sent by them.

Although Singapore's first Japanese resident, Yamamoto Otokichi (also known as John M. Ottoson), is known to have sunk his roots here in 1862, the island's nascent Japanese community only took shape after Japan lifted its ban on overseas travel following the Meiji Restoration of 1868.[4]

By the time the Straits Settlements population census of 1881 was carried out, there were 22 Japanese (8 male, 14 female) living in Singapore.[5] With the commencement of shipping routes from Japan to Bombay (present-day Mumbai) in 1893 and to various cities in Europe in 1896, the number of Japanese residents in Singapore began to grow, with people engaged in a variety of trades and occupations.

Some three decades later, the 1910 population census by the Japanese government recorded that the number of Japanese living in Singapore had risen to 1,215 residents, comprising professionals such as dentists and doctors, entrepreneurs like innkeepers and restaurant proprietors as well as photographers (PC82), hairdressers, plantation workers and those engaged in the sex trade (see table below).

CENSUS OF LOCAL JAPANESE BY PROFESSION IN 1910

Industry type	Number of businesses	Males	Females	Total no. of individuals
Sex work			353	353
Rubber industry	35	250	15	265
Brothels	80		73	73
Employed by foreigners			52	52
Food	12	23	11	34
Hairdressing	8	24	9	33
Board and lodging	9	15	14	29
Doctors	4	20	8	28
Pharmacy	6	23	2	25
Lodging	4	16	9	25
Dentistry	5	14	8	22
Food supplies and provision shops	5	16	5	21
Intermediaries	2	14	7	21
Laundry	4	14	4	18
Drapery	6	12	3	15
Official business (incl. servants)	3	10	4	14
Photography	3	7	6	13
Newspaper	2	10	3	13
Other business		111	50	161
Total	**188**	**579**	**636**	**1215**

Original data from the Ministry of Foreign Affairs' Archives. Translated from: The Japanese Association. (2016). シンガポール日本人社会百年史：星月夜の耀 [100 Year History of Japanese Community in Singapore (1915–2015)]. Singapore: The Japanese Association. (Call no.: RSING 305.895605957 ONE)

PC82
This postcard features
Hylam Street in Singapore.
On the right of the image is a
Japanese photography studio
called S.T. Yamato.
*Date and publisher
unknown. Accession no.:
B32440324K_0103*

At a time when economic migration tended to be the preserve of men, it is interesting to note that slightly more than half of Japanese residents in Singapore were women (636 women to 579 men). Of these female Japanese residents in Singapore, more than half were involved in sex work, who were known as *karayuki-san* ("women who have gone overseas"). Those not engaged in the sex trade worked in other sectors, such as food (e.g. restaurants), laundry, photography and newspaper publishing industries.[6]

First Impressions

What did these Japanese migrants see, feel and experience in this new land? PC83 provides a glimpse of a new arrival's first impressions of Singapore:

> We arrived [in] Singapore late last night. The five or six shadowy trees we saw above the reef were ones we had seen again and again on our journey here. Lit up against the setting sun, they were truly beautiful. It's pretty hot, and I am bewildered as to how it has changed from winter to summer in the span of half a month [...]

Church of Good Shepherd, Singapore.   No. 14

PC83
This postcard, featuring the Church of Good Shepherd in Singapore, is addressed to the Physics class at the Teachers' Training School in Tokyo. Besides recording his impressions of Singapore, the sender also notes that he will send more correspondence to the class.
Postmarked 18 March 1926.
Publisher unknown.
Accession no.:
B32413805D_0102

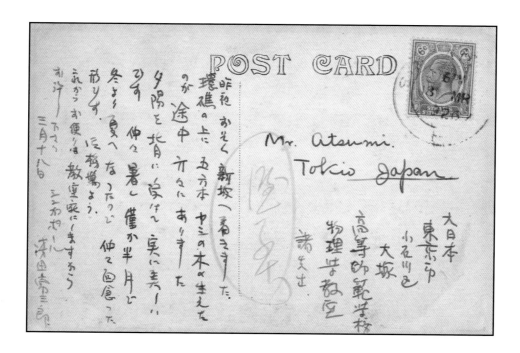

The confusion of PC83's writer would have been shared by his fellow travellers – they had just left Japan in March, when winter was ending, to a tropical climate with intense heat and humidity. Although some Japanese had already been living in Singapore since the 1860s, there was little, if any, existing travel literature in the early 20th century[7] to inform prospective visitors of Singapore's weather, culture or topography.

As such, wild stories were circulated about Singapore's searing heat, with tales of burnt and blackened corpses lying on the streets and natives wrapping their heads in white cloth to protect themselves from the sun.[8] Such impressions were eventually debunked after the new arrivals acclimatised to the tropical weather, and realised that the island's temperatures were actually similar to Japan's in the summer months.[9]

Prospective Japanese residents may have been surprised to discover how urbanised Singapore was. As their ships pulled into the harbour, tall buildings would have come into view, possibly overturning any preconceived notions of Singapore as a small fishing village. Presented with a thriving port city of the British empire, travellers might have wondered with "a sense of unease" as to what they had gotten themselves into.[10]

Setting Up Shop

The first Japanese provision shop, K. Nakagawa & Co., was set up in 1885, and sold Japanese goods and items at wholesale prices.[11] Such privately owned shops were a rarity during this period. In its first four years, K. Nakagawa & Co. (PC84) was the only Japanese provision shop in town until another opened in 1889.[12] During this time, the local Japanese community consisted largely of *karayuki-san* and brothel owners, hence, business proprietors chose to hire their new staff directly from Japan.[13]

In 1891, Mitsui & Co., a major Japanese trading company, established a branch in Singapore, marking a major turning point in the history of the local Japanese community and heralding the arrival of a new wave of Japanese professionals such as pharmacists and doctors.[14]

The opening of the first Japanese bank in Singapore, the Bank of Taiwan (under the auspices of the Japanese colonial administration in Taiwan), in 1912 (see PC46 and PC47 in Chapter 2) and shipping company Ōsaka Shōsen's introduction of a Singapore-based regional service that same year similarly ushered in the winds of change that swept over the local Japanese community.[15]

Figure 1
Echigoya was a Japanese draper's shop opened by Chubei Takahashi (seated) in 1907. Chubei was the proprietor in 1907 and is pictured here with his young Japanese staff.
The Japanese Association Singapore Collection, courtesy of National Archives of Singapore. Accession no.: 202384

Figure 2
Endo Takao, owner of the Tanjong Katong Rubber Estate perched on a tree in his plantation. Hoping to make their fortunes in booming industries such as rubber, many Japanese businessmen came to the region in search of business opportunities.

Source: 佃光治 [Tsukuda Mitsuharu]. (1917). *Marai ni okeru hōjin katsudō no genkyō* [Current Status of the Activities of Japanese in Malaya]. Singapore: Nanyō oyobi Nihonjinsha, p. 28. (Call no.: RRARE 305.89560595 TSU-[LSB]). Also available on BookSG.

These professionals not only provided services and supplies to the Japanese community residing in Singapore (such as textiles, see Figure 1) but also hosted friends visiting from Japan (PC89). Japanese business proprietors who were already comfortably settled in Singapore also set up new industries (such as rubber, see Figure 2), on the island. For instance, Ōkawa Kiyotachi was responsible for bringing over the first group of fishermen from Chiba Prefecture to begin a new fishing business in Singapore. This subsequently led to the arrival of more Japanese fishermen between 1892 and 1895, including some 61 men from regions such as Wakayama Prefecture.[16]

H. No. 328 High Street Singapore

PC84
Visible on the left of the
postcard is the first Japanese
provision shop in Singapore,
K. Nakagawa, which was
located at 328 High Street.
*Date unknown. Publisher:
M.S.N. Co. Accession no.:
B32413806E_0104*

The Lim Shao Bin Collection contains another interesting set of postcards and letters containing business correspondence (PC85–88) – these were sent by Ejiri Koichirō, the owner of K. Ejiri, a Japanese pharmacy located at 414 North Bridge Road in Singapore. He had corresponded with his acquaintance, Tajika Shōjiro, who was also from the pharmaceutical industry, between 1909 and 1925. Their correspondence recorded the various places where Tajika lived and worked over this 16-year period: from Suzhou, China in 1909 (PC85) to Toyama City, Japan in 1912 (PC86) to Seremban, Malaysia in 1918 (PC87); and finally back to Toyama City in 1925 (PC88).

Ejiri's postcards are useful for understanding how a new Japanese migrant may have settled into life in Singapore. PC85 stands out from the other correspondence sent by Ejiri, as it is the only one that does not bear the company stamp "K. Ejiri". Moreover, the address indicated on the postcard is 14 Middle Road (written in both *katakana* and *kanji* characters), and not 414 North Bridge Road, which was the address used on both the company's stamp and letterhead between 1912 and 1925. Being the earliest postcard in the lot, it suggests that Ejiri had moved to Singapore by 1909 and had not set up his business yet.[17]

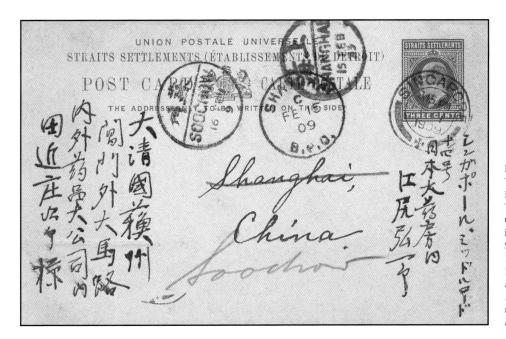

PC85
This postcard was from Ejiri Koichirō in Singapore to Tajika Shōjiro in Suzhou, China. This government-issued postcard reached Shanghai on 15 February 1909 and Suzhou on 16 February 1909. *Postmarked 1 February 1909 (Singapore). Publisher unknown. Accession no.: B32413805D_0005*

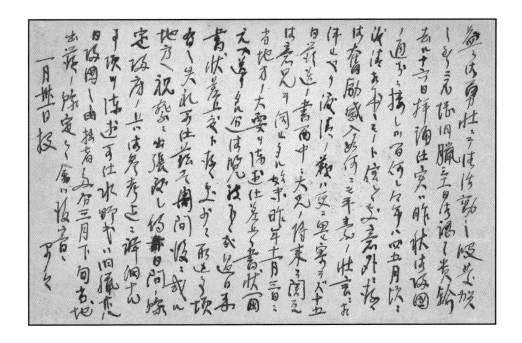

PC86
This postcard was sent by Ejiri Koichiro, now located at 414 North Bridge Road in Singapore, to Tajika Shōjiro, in Toyama Prefecture. The sender, Ejiri, writes that he is departing Singapore on the 31st of the following month, on the *Tamba-maru*, with a stopover at Osaka for four to five days. On his return home, he indicates he would like to stay with the Shioda family so there would be no need to look for a house to rent. *Postmarked 16 October 1912. Publisher unknown. Accession no.: B32413805D_0008*

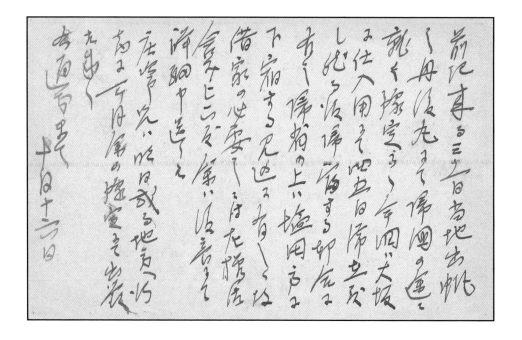

PC87
Here, Ejiri Koichirō sends a letter instead of a postcard to Tajika Shōjiro, who had relocated to Seremban in the Federated Malay States. In his letter, Ejiri writes about the Japanese and Chinese medical supplies that were sold in the store. The letter was sent from the post office that used to operate from Raffles Hotel.
Postmarked 17 May 1918.
Accession no.:
B32413805D_0013

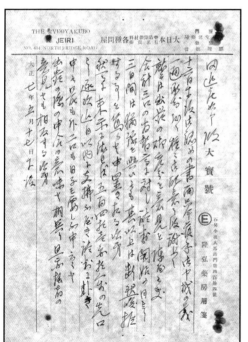

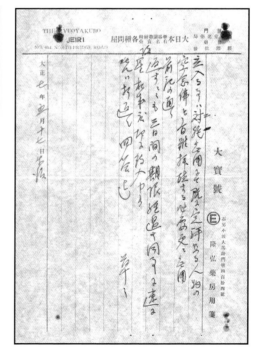

PC88
This correspondence was from Ejiri Koichirō to Tajika Shōjiro in Toyama City, Japan. The English address states "Kobe, Japan", but the Japanese address indicates "Toyama Prefecture, Toyama City". *Postmarked 1925. Accession no.: B32413805D_0011*

Tokyo: Nihonbashi Broadway.

東京日本橋通

PC89
Featuring Nihonbashi Broadway in Tokyo, this postcard was sent to K. Ejiri from Fukujima Tōsaku who had visited Ejiri in Singapore. On the reverse of the postcard is a stock message to inform Ejiri, and others who had hosted Fukujima during his travels, that he had returned safely to Japan, as well as to thank him for his hospitality.
Dated April 1923. Publisher unknown. Accession no.: B32413805D_0100

JAPANESE DISPENSARY
Dr. NISHIMURA
Open every day from 8 a m. to 6 p.m.
Consulting hours 7 a.m. to 5 p.m.
No. 14 Middle Road,
June 10   SINGAPORE.   μιwf 9.12

The property at Middle Road, "a cozy and fine three-story house with cheap rent", is a particularly interesting location, as the aforementioned Japanese resident Dr Nishimura Takeshirō had first set up his dispensary there (see Figure 3) before moving to new premises in 1906.[18] After Dr Nishimura moved out, the property was leased by Endō Takao, the proprietor of Navy Hotel located at 5-17 Beach Road.[19]

It appears that 14 Middle Road was not only a popular location for newcomers due to its affordable rent and proximity to the Japanese merchant district, but also its potential for networking within the local Japanese community. While it is unclear if Ejiri took over the lease from Endo or was only temporarily residing with him, 14 Middle Road was likely a useful location in helping Ejiri to establish his network and contacts in Singapore. The North Bridge Road and Middle Road areas, including adjacent streets such as Malay and Malabar streets, were commonly known as Little Japan.[20]

The rubber boom from 1906 also brought in workers and investors eager to reap profits (see Chapter 2).[21] However, when the global demand for rubber fell and prices plunged in the years following the First World War, the effects rippled through Singapore's Japanese community: the population fell from 3,591 individuals in 1920 to 1,731 in 1924.[22] Although rubber prices rebounded in 1925, they plummeted again in 1930 at the onset of the Great Depression, falling by almost 40 percent within a year.[23]

Even so, the steep decline in the number of Japanese residents between 1920 and 1925 was not solely due to the crash in the rubber market and weak global economy. In 1920, an abolition edict issued by Japan's Acting-Consul in Singapore came into effect, resulting in the expulsion of *karayuki-san* from the island.[24] To understand the lead-up to this, it is useful to examine the circumstances that brought these women to Singapore.

ISHIHARA AND CO.

Ishihara and Co., located at 14 and 15 Winchester House and 16 Collyer Quay, was a trading company engaged in the export of tropical produce such as rubber, tin, sago powder, gambier, rattan, pepper and tapioca, and the import of industrial products such as steel wire ropes, machinery, hardware, automobiles, tires, galvanised pipes, shovels, copper boat nails, paints, red leads and carbides.⁺

PC90 was sent by Ishihara G. of Ishihara and Co. to Uno Kazuo of Kyodo Commercial Co. Ltd in Java, noting that Singapore had experienced a lot of rainfall. Ishihara and Co. was also one of several businesses that participated in the fundraising efforts for the commissioning of Sir Arthur Young's portrait, then-governor of the Straits Settlements, in 1919 (Figure 4), and a wedding gift for Princess Mary of the British royal family on the occasion of her marriage to Viscount Lascelles in 1922 (Figure 5).*

Sir Arthur Young's Portrait Fund.

The committee gratefully acknowledge receipt of the following subscriptions.—

Amount previously acknowledged $3,180.

$100 each.—Ban Heng Lee, Huay Thong, Choo U Lan, Lam Wah, Guan Chin Hong, Heap Hust, Heap Eng Moh Steamship Company, East Indies Trading Company.

$10 each.—Lee Hong Leong, Kum Ching Soo, Dr. N. L. Clarke, J. G Hubback, Lee Pang Seng, Choa Eng Wan, S. K. Wong, Rahamin Penhas, Oguia and Co., Ltd, Ishihara and Co, Siemens Brothers Dynamo Works, Ltd., H. C. Cooke-Yarborough, C. F. Brown, Yow Ngan Pan, Otomune and Co., Ltd., The East Asiatic Company Ltd., Mount Austin (Johore) Rubber Estates Ltd., H. Wolskel, Adda Rubber Estates, Johore, Timor Rubber Estates, Johore, Straits Times Press, Ltd., H M. Ware, O. P. Griffith Jones, R. R. Turner, Behr and Co., Trading Company "Holland," W. M. Franke, Sturzenegger and Co., The Malaya Tribune, McAlister and Co., Limited, W. P. Plummer, D. J. Ward, A. W. Vick, F. S. Newell, Justice P. J Sproule, L. Molteni, United Malaysian Rubber Co.

$5 each.—E. Tessensohn, C. A. da Silva, H. S. Finck, Anonymous, Nunoi Shoten, W. M. Baker.

$2 each.—A.H.C, T.K.S., C. V. Ganno.

$1 each.—N. B. Westerhout, C.A.S., A. S.

Total $4,889.

Subscriptions which may be of any amount up to but not exceeding $10 should be sent to the Chartered Bank, Singapore.

This applies to individual subscriptions not to subscriptions from associations, firms and clubs, as to which there is no limit.

Figure 4

Princess Mary's Wedding.

Dollar Subscription for A Present.

The marriage of Princess Mary to Viscount Lascelles takes place on the 28th inst. and it is felt that Malaya should take the opportunity of shewing its loyal and affectionate esteem for the Royal Family by sending a gift to the Princess on that happy occasion. Prosperity does not abound with us, and there is no wish that any members of the community should feel that a heavy call is being made upon them. What is desired is that the largest possible number should join in the gift and that the contribution should be of such a nominal amount as to be in no sense a burden to anyone.

Therefore, with the full assent of those in authority, we are asking for subscriptions of one dollar, and we suggest that the maximum be five dollars, for any one individual's subscription.

As time is very short we pray the favour of a prompt response from all who desire to participate.

We are very grateful indeed to the heads of several firms who have kindly undertaken to bring the matter to the notice of their staffs.

	$	cts.
Already Acknowledged ..	143	40
Ishihara and Co., Singapore :— Messrs. H. Ishihara, G. Ishihara, S. Ishihara, H. Nakagawa, T. Murai, T. Yamashita, K. Gotoh, Y. Nakatsuka, M. Kubo, Khoo Beng Watt, each $1=$10. ..	10	00
Capt. E. P. Richards ..	5	00

Figure 5

⁺ Sources: Untitled [Microfilm: NL 1657]. (1921, June 21). *The Singapore Free Press and Mercantile Advertiser*, p. 4; Notice [Microfilm: NL 00519]. (1924, June 6). *The Straits Times*, p. 7.; New Stock Just Arrived [Microfilm: NL 00450]. (1918, December 7). *The Straits Times*, p. 5.; Toyko Seiko Kaisha [Microfilm: NL 00453]. (1919, March 28). *The Straits Times*, p. 7; 南洋協会(Japan). 新嘉坡商品陳列館 [Nanyō Kyōkai (Japan). Shingapōru shōhin chinretsukan]. (1920). *南洋之産業. 壹之巻* [Nanyō no sangyō. Ichi no ken]. Singapore: Shingapōru Shōhin Chinretsukan, p. 234. (Call no.: RRARE 338.0959 NAN) Digitised book available from BookSG.

*Sources: Sir Arthur Young's portrait [Microfilm: NL 2121]. (1919, December 8). *The Singapore Free Press and Mercantile Advertiser*, p. 7.; Princess Mary's wedding [Microfilm: NL 491]. (1922, February 11). *The Straits Times*, p. 8.

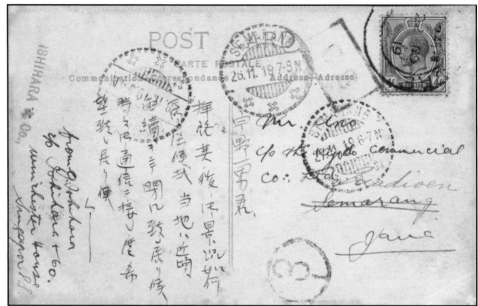

PC90
Featuring a boy on a durian tree, this postcard was
sent by G. Ishihara c/o Ishihara and Co., Winchester
House, Singapore to Kazuo Uno of the Kyodo
Commercial Co. Ltd, Java. In it, Ishihara asks Uno
how things are in Java. He says that Singapore has
experienced a lot of rain; and that it will be good to
hear from Uno soon. The address was found to be
incorrect and the postcard was redirected (location
illegible) on 28 November 1919.
*Postmarked 22 November 1919 (Singapore). Publisher
unknown. Accession no.: B32413805D_0079*

Karayuki-san

Many *karayuki-san* were from the poor, rural parts of Kyushu island in Japan. Caught in seemingly unending cycles of poverty, desperate families sold their daughters to pimps who trafficked them as prostitutes in foreign lands. In Japan's traditional patrilineal society, daughters were generally viewed as dispensable commodities, to be given away in marriage when the time came. Given the lowly status of women, selling a girl off – especially when a family had one too many daughters – was not an uncommon practice.[25] Yet not all *karayuki-san* were sold into bondage. Others were kidnapped and forced into the sex trade.[26] In 1905, a brothel owner in Singapore who ran an establishment with six girls could rake in as much as 18,000 yen per year, with each girl earning about 250 yen a month.[27] In comparison, a police constable in Japan in 1906 would have drawn a starting salary of 17 yen per month (or 204 yen per annum).[28]

By the late Meiji era (1868–1912), Singapore had become notorious for its large number of *karayuki-san*.[29] The presence of these women reflected the high demand for their services in a colonial port city populated mostly by young, single migrant men. Due to a lack of financial means or existing immigration laws (often a combination of both), many male migrants were unable to bring their partners from back home or establish families of their own in the countries they settled in. For them, the services of *karayuki-san* were a welcome, if fleeting, distraction from the drudgery of their daily lives.[30]

PC91 and PC92 offer an insight into the correspondence that a customer might have had with a *karayuki-san*. Written in the same hand, both these postcards were addressed to Miss K. Yamamoto, c/o 25 Malay Street (which ran adjacent to Middle Road), Singapore. If the postcards did reach Miss K. Yamamoto, they were likely delivered by hand, since the postcards bear no postage stamps. It is likely that Miss K. Yamamoto was a *karayuki-san* and the writer of the postcard was her patron.

Drawn by the prospects of good money as well as a means of publicity for their sexual services, or perhaps out of sheer vanity, some *karayuki-san* also modelled at the request of enterprising Chinese and European photographers working in Singapore, posing in their *kimono* for photographs that were eventually printed on postcards (such as PC93).[31] Although the woman pictured on PC93 cannot be definitively identified as a *karayuki-san*, the absence of a white trim on her collar and her low *obi* (a sash for

PC91
Featuring farm houses in
Singapore, this postcard
was addressed to Miss K.
Yamamoto, most likely a
karayuki-san, c/o No. 25,
Malay Street, a building
which operated both as a
Japanese
eatery and brothel.
*Date and publisher
unknown. Accession no.:
B32413805D_0119*

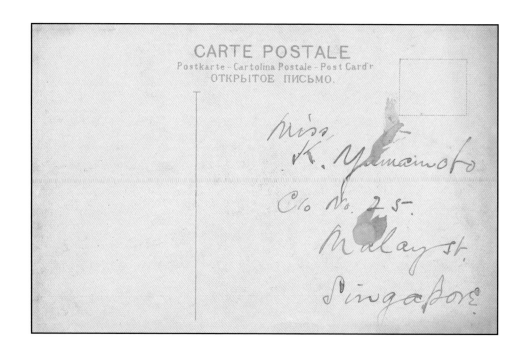

(87)   Selangoon Road, Singapore.

PC92
This postcard featuring
Selangoon [sic] Road
in Singapore was also
addressed to Miss K.
Yamamoto c/o No. 25, Malay
Street. The absence of a
postage stamp suggests that
these postcards might have
been delivered by hand to
Miss Yamamoto.
*Date and publisher
unknown. Accession no:.
B32413805D_0120*

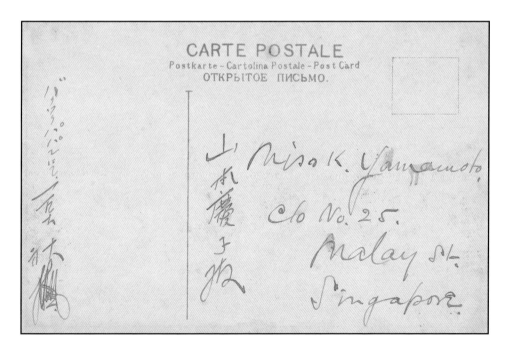

the *kimono*) suggests that she was one. According to James Warren, "unmarried young ladies from good families" typically had their *obi* wrapped tightly over their breasts to show "proper upbringing". The white trim emphasised their purity (for example, PC94); hence the absence of these elements in the *kimono* of the Japanese women on some of these postcards mark them as likely to be *karayuki-san*.[32]

Such postcards would have fostered the impressions travellers had of Singapore "as a centre of romanticism, exoticism, and easy sex", represented by the image of the Japanese woman clad in traditional Japanese dress.[33] Regardless of whether the women were indeed *karayuki-san*, or even living in Singapore, that postcards PC95–98 were bought and sent to friends and family suggest that these Japanese ladies were part of early travellers' impressions of Singapore. After all, the Malay Street quarter, where most *karayuki-san* in Singapore operated, was not far from Raffles Hotel and other famous accommodations such as Hotel de l'Europe.[34]

Some hotels were also directly involved with *karayuki-san*. Matsuo Ryokan, located on Malabar Street (which intersected Malay Street and ran adjacent to Middle Road), was an inn that enjoyed the patronage of illustrious personalities such as Natsume Sōseki, considered Japan's greatest writer of modern literature, and Kuroda Seiki, one of the leaders of the Western-style painting movement in Japan.[35] However, Matsuo Ryokan also appeared to have been operating as a brothel on the side, providing temporary lodgings for impoverished Japanese women who had been forced to become *karayuki-san*. In fact, the inn seemed to have made specific arrangements for horse-drawn carriages to pick the women up once they arrived at the port.[36]

Although *karayuki-san* might have been a major attraction for tourists and men seeking the pleasures of the night, they became a source of embarrassment for the growing Japanese community.[37] In the early 20th century, Japanese firms began making their way to Singapore, introducing a new wave of white-collar workers who were socioeconomically different from the *karayuki-san* who formed part of the earliest wave of Japanese migration to Singapore. Ashamed of these women and keen to rid themselves of this perceived blemish on the reputation of the Japanese, some prominent members of the local Japanese community sought to eradicate the presence of *karayuki-san* in Singapore.

Despite initial setbacks, the movement soon gained momentum under the auspices of the Japanese government, which was also keen on the abolition of *karayuki-san* in order to enhance its reputation among economically powerful Western nations.[38] Under the active lobbying of the acting Japanese Consul-General in Singapore, Yamazaki Heikichi, the abolition edict was passed in 1920, leaving the *karayuki-san* scrambling to make alternative arrangements: either to return to Japan, or remain in Singapore as servants or as wives to men in Singapore.[39]

It was a miserable situation for many *karayuki-san* and one that was doubly unjust given that these women were one of the reasons that the fledgling Japanese community in Singapore had grown. For Japan, which was in desperate need of overseas funds to stimulate its economy, the presence of *karayuki-san* had enabled small Japanese businesses to establish themselves in Singapore and other Asian countries.[40] Despite the abolition edict, some Japanese sex workers and brothels in Singapore continued to operate illegally after 1920, and even into the 1930s.[41] These clandestine operations were carried out at Japanese hotels or boarding houses, with proprietors harbouring girls under the pretence that they were guests or boarders.[42]

Karayuki-san were not only notable for their economic contributions, they were also actively involved in disaster relief efforts in Japan, sending essential items such as *yukata* (a lighter variation of the *kimono* made of cotton) and bedding home in response to rallying calls for emergency supplies.[43] It is also likely that some of these women periodically sent money and goods to their impoverished families in Japan. Far from being parasites, these women not only helped spur the growth of the Japanese community in Singapore but also boosted the domestic economy in Japan. Sadly, they were never fully accepted in either country. Gazing out of these picture postcards, they were to remain as objects of curiosity and sexual fantasy, rather than individuals with personalities and stories of their own.

Singapore. Japanese lady.

PC93
This postcard features a Japanese lady in Singapore, likely a *karayuki-san*, in her *kimono*. *Karayuki-san* sometimes posed for photographs at the request of photographers in Singapore.
Date and publisher unknown.
Accession no.: B32440324K_0076

PC94
This postcard of a Japanese lady in Singapore features a painted background of what appears to be a hut and tropical palm trees. The collar of her kimono is embellished with a white trim, indicating that she is not a *karayuki-san*.
Date and publisher unknown.
Accession no.: B32440324K_0075

Singapore. Japanese lady.

PC95
Bound for Paris, this postcard presents three Japanese women in traditional clothes posing with traditional Chinese and Japanese instruments. The instruments (from left) are a *koto, kokyū* and *gekkin*. Although the publisher is not indicated on the postcard, the same decorative border on the backs of both PC95 and PC96 suggests that the two are from the same publisher. *Postmarked 4 December 1905, but message dated 5 December 1905. Publisher unknown. Accession no.: B32440324K_0073*

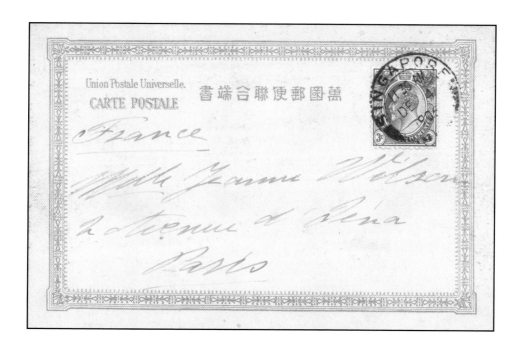

PC96
The Japanese woman featured in this
postcard is playing the *shamisen*. Similar
to PC95, this postcard was also bound
for Paris and bears a 3-cent Straits
Settlements stamp.
Dated 1904. Publisher unknown.
Accession no.: B32440324K_0074

PC97
This postcard features a *maiko* (geisha-in-training) playing a *shime-daiko* (referred to as a *taiko* [a drum] in the postcard). This was a New Year's greeting card, written in English and sent to Petersham, Massachusetts from Singapore.
Postmarked 5 February 1904 (Boston, Massachusetts). Publisher unknown. Accession no.: B32413805D_0035

PC98
This postcard presents a Japanese
woman in a kimono. The sender
reassures the postcard's recipient
that they have not been forgotten.
*Dated 4 February 1904 (postmarked
Singapore). Publisher unknown.
Accession no.: B32413805D_0036*

Notes

1   For a further discussion of Japanese migration to Southeast Asia, see Befu, H. (2010) "Japanese Transnational Migration in Time and Space: An Historical Overview" in *Japanese and Nikkei at Home and Abroad: Negotiating Identities in a Global World*, edited by Nobuko, A. New York: Cambria Press. (Not available in NLB holdings)

2   The fourth son of a family of five, Dr Nishimura Takeshirō graduated from Osaka Medical School and worked at Tokyo Medical University's Department of Surgery for four years before opening his own practice in 1902. Upon arriving in Singapore, he first set up an small dispensary at Daiwa Inn, before relocating to larger quarters at 14 Middle Road. Intriguingly, Nishimura was less inclined to work with Japanese patients in Singapore than with Chinese patients, a direction motivated by his conviction that the best way to "edify China" was through medicine. He subsequently moved to Hill Street, where his target demographic, the Chinese community, was found in larger numbers. Nishimura was frequently at loggerheads with Nakano Kōzō, the first Japanese doctor in Singapore, over Nishimura's work with the Chinese. 西村竹四郎 [Nishimura Takeshirō]. *(1911)*. 在南三十五年 [Zainan sanjūgo nen]. Tōkyō: Ankyūsha, pp. 3–4, 25–26, 57–58, 65, 147, 155, 219–220. (Not available in NLB holdings)

3   Nishimura, 1911, p. 572.

4   For more information on John M. Ottoson, see Leong, F. M. (2012). *John M. Ottoson: Later career of Otokichi*. Singapore: Heritage Committee, Japanese Association Singapore. (Call no.: RSING 959.5703092 LEO) ; See also 音吉顕彰会 [Otokichikenshōkai]. (2006). 音吉の足跡を追って：草の根活動の15年 [Otokichi no sokuseki o otte : kusa no ne katsudō no 15 nen]. Miha-chō, Japan: Aichikenshō kai. (Call no.: RSING 920.710952 OTO)

5   Census Office. (1881). *Report on the census of the Straits Settlements, taken on the 3rd April 1881*. Singapore: Census Office, p. 1. Retrieved from Singapore Memory Project website, also available on BookSG; see also 南洋及び日本人社 [Nanyō oyobi Nipponjinsha]. (1938). シンガポールを中心に同胞活躍—南洋の50年 [Shingapōru wo chūshin ni dōhō katsuyaku – Nanyō no 50 nen]. Singapore: Nanyō oyobi Nipponjinsha, p. 522. (Call no.: RSING 959.004956 NAN)

6   The Japanese Association. (2016). シンガポール日本人社会百年史：星月夜の耀 [100 Year History of Japanese Community in Singapore (1915–2015)]. Singapore: The Japanese Association, p. 32. (Call no.: RSING 305.895605957 ONE)

7   The earliest known Japanese travel guidebook on Singapore, *Shingapōru annai* (The Guide Book of Singapore, or Harada's Guide), was published in 1919, so travellers visiting the country before then were largely in the dark about what Singapore was like. It was published by Johdai Printing Works, located at No. 50 Bras Basah Road in Singapore.

8   Nishimura, 1911, p. 14.

9   Nishimura, 1911, p. 15.

10 Nishimura, 1911, p. 15.

11 The Japanese Association, 2016, p. 22, 34.

12 K. Nakagawa and Co. remained open until at least 1910, when it published an advertisement, see The Japanese Association, 2016, p. 22.

13 Tsu, Y.H. (2006). A social history. In Tsu, Y.H. (Ed.), *Japan and Singapore: A Multidisciplinary Approach*. Singapore: McGraw-Hill Education, p. 25. (Call no.: RSING 303.4825205957 JAP); The Japanese Association, 2016, p. 22.

14 Tsu, 2006, pp. 29–30.

15 Tsu, 2006, p. 30.

16 The Japanese Association, 2016, p. 24.

17 シンガポール日本人クラブ [Shingapōru Nihonjin Kurabu]. (1939). 赤道を歩く [Sekidō wo aruku]. Tokyo: Dainihon Insatsu Busshi Kaisha, p. 49 (of advertisement pullout). (Not available in NLB holdings)

18 Nishimura, 1911, p. 26, 65.

19 A search for "T. Endo" using NewspaperSG does not turn up any advertisements or articles prior to 1906, suggesting that he had only begun running the hotel then.

20 Blackburn, K. (2007). "Heritage site, war memorial, and tourist stop: The Japanese Cemetery of Singapore, 1891–2005" in *Journal of the Malaysian Branch of the Royal Asiatic Society* 80.1: 17–39. Kuala Lumpur: Malaysian Branch, Royal Asiatic Society. (Call no.: RSING 959.5 JMBRAS–[LKY])

21 Nishimura, 1911, pp. 78–79.

22 The Japanese Association, 2016, p. 86.

23 The rubber prices that Nishimura lists in 1930 show a steep drop from 25 cents at the start of the year to 15 cents on 4 December. Nishimura, 1911, pp. 412–13, 537–38.

24 The Japanese Acting Consul-General Yamazaki gathered Japanese representatives from all over Singapore to inform them of the decision to abolish prostitution on 4 January 1920. 西原大輔 [Daisuke Nishihara]. (2017). 幕末明治から日本占領下・戦後まで [Nihonjin no Shingapōru Taiken: Bakumatsumeiji kara nihonsenryōka.sengo made]. Kyoto: Jinbun Shoin, p. 103. (Not available in NLB holdings)

25 Warren, J. (1993). *Ah Ku and Karayuki-san: Prostitution in Singapore*. Singapore: National University Press, pp. 25, 30. (Call no.: RSING 306.74095957 WAR)

26 Warren, 1993, pp. 82–83.

27 Warren, 1993, p. 61.

28 Shūkan Asahi (ed.) (1998). *Nedanshi nenpyō*. Tokyo: Asahi Shimbunsha, p. 91. (Not available in NLB holdings)

29 Warren, 1993, p. 41.

30 Warren, 1993, p. 33.

31 Warren, 1993, p. 252. PC93 is also featured in Warren, 1993, picture 21a.

32 Warren, 1993, p. 251.

33 Warren, 1993, p. 252.

34 Warren, 1993, p. 269.

35 Nishihara, 2017, pp. 55–57.

36 Nishimura, 1911, p. 14.

37 Tsu, 2006, p. 29.

38 Warren, 1993, p. 164.

39 Social service committee: fruits of its labour [Microfilm: NL 1648]. (1920, January 13). *The Singapore Free Press and Mercantile Advertiser*, p. 12.; 南洋及び日本人社 [Nanyō oyobi Nipponjinsha], 1938, p. 149; See also Mihalopoulos, B. (2011). *Sex in Japan's globalization, 1870–1930: Prostitutes, emigration and nation*. New York: Routledge. (Call no.: RSING 306.7420952 MIH)

40 Warren, 1993, p. 35, 62.

41 Immorality [Microfilm: NL 3886]. (1930, June 14). *Malaya Tribune*, p. 7.

42 Sly brothel menace: boarding house keeper charged [Microfilm: NL 516.] (1924, March 13). *The Straits Times*, p. 9.

43 The Japanese Association, 2016, p. 48.

SUPPLEMENTARY POSTCARDS

PC99
Shopfronts along High Street in Singapore – many Japanese businesses were clustered around this area.
Date unknown and publisher unknown. Accession no.: B32413806E_0102

High Street, Singapore

PC100
High Street was home to a variety of shops, such as the Japanese shop Kiyono & Co., as well as A.T. Ramchand Bros (also on the right), which imported Fuji silk for dressmaking. *Date unknown. Publisher unknown. Accession no.: B32413806E_0105*

High Street, Singapore

PC101
This postcard presents an aerial view of High Street. Atop Fort Canning Hill in the background are a flagstaff and lighthouse. *Date unknown. Publisher unknown. Accession no.: B32413806E_0106*

PC102
Visible in the middle of the postcard is a Japanese shop called The Nansei Co. The shop appears to have sold laces, fancy goods and curios.
Date unknown. Publisher unknown. Accession no.: B32413806E_0107

PC103
Japanese characters can be seen on the cane-shaped signboard in the middle of the left row of shops on the postcard, suggesting that this shop sold walking sticks.
Date unknown. Publisher unknown. Accession no.: B32413806E_0108

PC104
Addressed to Brighton,
England, to "dearest
Kathleen from Freddie", this
postcard features a woman
in traditional Japanese
dress serving rice.
*Dated 2 June 1905
(postmarked Singapore).
Publisher unknown.
Accession no.:
B32413805D_0040*

PC105
This postcard doubling as a Christmas card features morning glory flowers and a girl wearing traditional Japanese dress and a headscarf. *Postmarked December 1902 (Singapore). Publisher unknown. Accession no: B32413805D_0032*

OSTALE

Postale -- Post Card

ПИСЬМО.

CHAPTER 4

CIRCULATION OF JAPANESE POSTCARDS IN SINGAPORE

In this final chapter, we move from postcards as historical objects to the social history behind postcards, specifically the study of how postcards were produced and used by the Japanese community in Singapore.

Producing and Circulating Postcards in Singapore

One of the earliest Japanese photography studios to produce picture postcards in Singapore was Togo & Co., which began producing and selling postcards in the early 1900s. Figure 1 shows its premises as well as a portrait likely to be of its studio manager, Mitsui Toshimasa.[1] Postcards from this studio typically depicted local buildings such as Hindu temples (PC106), local flora and fauna (PC107 and PC108), local industries such as rubber tapping, as well as hotels and places of interest (see PC31 in Chapter 2), suggesting that such subjects might have been popular with consumers.

Togo & Co. also photographed and produced commemorative picture postcards marking important community events. One example was the founding of Saiyūji Temple[2] at Yio Chu Kang in Singapore in 1911 by Hioki Mokusen. Hioki was a renowned Zen monk who later became the 66th chief abbot of Eihei-ji, one of Japan's main Zen temples.[3]

Singapore's much-acclaimed photography studio G.R. Lambert & Co., which was established in 1867, was also a pioneer – it had been selling a series of postcards bearing images of Japanese women.[4]

Figure 1
The premises of Togo &
Co., or Togo Photographers
(Togo Shashinkan). The text
on the left of the postcard
notes "Mitsui Toshimasa
was not only involved in the
photography, but also with
the cultivation
of rubber."

Source: Tomojiro Itō. (1914).
*Nanyō Guntō Shashin Gachō:
Fu Nanyō Jijō* [Picture book
of the South Sea Islands].
Eiryō Penan Shi: Nanyō
chōsakai, p. 21.
(Call no.: RRARE 959 ITO)

In 1902, an unnamed company circulated PC105 (Chapter 3), which featured a woman in Japanese dress and a decorated border, which does not appear to have been produced in Singapore. PC97, PC98 and PC104 (Chapter 3) similarly share the same border, suggesting that they were produced by the same company. The consumers of such postcards were not only tourists but also local Japanese residents, Sugino Reisuku being one example. Sugino, an employee with the branch office of Mitsui & Co. (a trading company) in Singapore, had used such a postcard when writing to a Japanese acquaintance.[5]

Gradually, photographers began to take an interest in subjects beyond local buildings, events and people. Takahashi Shōhei, who took over Togo & Co. in 1917[6] and renamed it Daiwa Photography Studio, was most interested in photographing the activities of the local Japanese community in Singapore. Many of Takahashi's photographs appear in the book *Marai ni okeru hōjin katsudō no genkyō* (Current Status of the Activities of the Japanese in Malaya), which was published by Nanyō Oyobi Nipponjin Sha (South Seas and the Japanese Press).[7]

H 238   The Hindu Temple. Singapore.

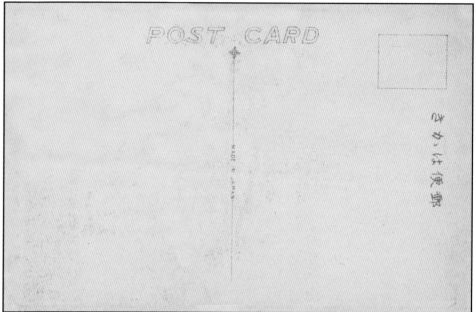

POST CARD

MADE IN JAPAN

きかゝは便郵

PC106
This made-in-Japan postcard
features the Sri Mariamman
Temple at South Bridge Road.
*Date unknown. Publisher: Togo
& Co. Printing. Accession no.:
B32413805D_0145*

JUST RIPENED COCOANUTS

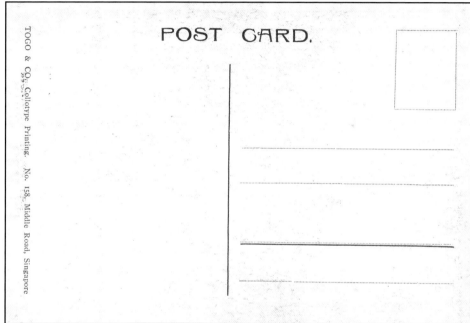

POST CARD.

TOGO & CO., Collotype Printing. No. 158, Middle Road, Singapore

PC107
This postcard featuring ripened
coconuts was produced by Togo
& Co. Postcards like this gave its
recipients an idea of tropical produce
found in Singapore.
*Date unknown. Publisher: Togo
& Co. Printing. Accession no.:
B32413807F_0160*

ONKANG.   SINGAPORE.

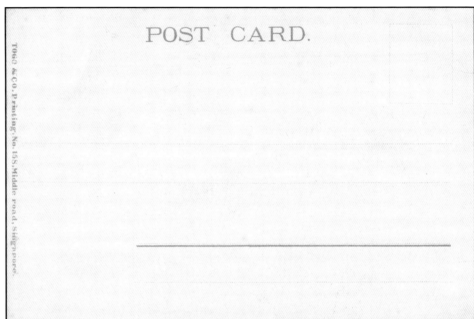

PC108
Produced by Togo & Co., postcards
such as this one presenting a close-
up of a monkey reinforced ideas of
Singapore as an exotic destination.
*Date unknown. Publisher: Togo
& Co. Printing. Accession no.:
B32440324K_0012*

An interesting inclusion in Takahashi's book is the photograph of a large snake (PC109), together with the description "23 metres in length (and) the swollen belly suggests that it had swollen [*sic*] a deer".[8] The image is part of a series of photographs, titled *A Big Snake Swallowing a Deer*, that was made into picture postcards. The photograph on PC109 captures the snake hissing in fury at the camera; PC110 presents the snake tied to a pole; PC111 shows the dead snake surrounded by a group of beaming men who were presumably part of the hunt; and the picture on PC112 shows the deer that was pried out of the snake's stomach. Obviously, there was a market for postcards depicting such exotica in Singapore.

TRIANGLE SPACES FOR STAMPS

According to Chai Foh Chin's *Early Picture Postcards of North Borneo and Labuan*, the unusual triangular space marked out for stamps on the back of some early postcards were thought to be a distinctive feature used by a group of some 50 Japanese photographers and artists in the 1920s. Postcards PC110, PC111 and PC112 were likely to have been produced by Takahashi Shōhei, and suggests that he was part of this group. See pages 179–190 for more postcards with such triangle spaces for stamps.

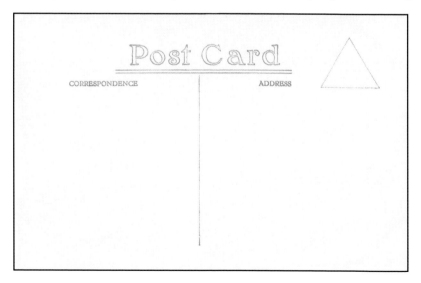

Source: Chai, F. C. (2007). *Early Picture Postcards of North Borneo and Labuan*. Kota Kinabalu: Opus Publications, p. 2. (Call no.: RSING 959.53 CHA)

PC109
This set of four images (PC109–112), later turned into postcards, were from a series called *A Big Snake Swallowing a Deer*. They were published in *Marai ni okeru hōjin katsudō no genkyō* (Current Status of the Activities of the Japanese in Malaya). This postcard features the python with its belly swollen with its prey (a deer). The image was taken at the Fujita Kumi Plantation. *Date and publisher unknown. Accession no.: B32413807F_0149*

PC110
A group of men, presumably the hunting party, pose for a picture with the python, which had been strapped onto a pole after being caught. *Date and publisher unknown. Accession no.: B32413807F_0146*

PC111
The dead python, with its extended belly, is laid on the ground prior to being cut open.
Undated and publisher unknown. Accession no.: B32413807F_0147

PC112
This postcard features the deer after it was extracted from the stomach of the python.
Date and publisher unknown. Accession no.: B32413807F_0150

Located at 168 Middle Road, Kōbunkan was another Japanese company that produced postcards during this period (see pages 173–177). It released a series of postcards titled *Shingapōru Fukei Ehagaki* (Singapore Landscapes on Postcards).[9] Apart from postcards, Kōbunkan also published *Nanyō Sōran* (A Guide to Nanyō) in 1920,[10] which featured the customs and religions of the local people, modes of transport, trades and Japanese businesses in Singapore. Kōbunkan also sold Japanese and Western-style postcards, newspapers, books, maps, stationery, canned food and was a major retailer of the Sakura brand of beer.[11]

Besides companies and studios, there were also private individuals producing postcards in Singapore. Inoue Takefumi, an illustrator for *Nanyō Puck* (a locally produced satirical manga magazine), privately published a series of lithographic coloured picture postcards that featured local scenery, animals and tropical fruits.[12]

Commemorative Souvenirs

Postcards were also purchased as souvenirs of Singapore by visitors from Japan, including Japanese naval fleets on their stopovers here. Packaged together with local sweetmeats in a hamper, they were presented to naval officers for distribution to their crew members.[13] The postcards presented to the naval personnel do not appear to have been specially created, but rather, were ordinary picture postcards inked with special commemorative stamps to mark the occasion (such as PC113 and PC114).[14]

Apart from functioning as memorabilia, visiting naval officers also used picture postcards as visual aids in the reports they prepared for their superiors in Japan. For instance, PC113, which features the Raffles Library and Museum, was addressed to Baron Saitō Makoto (Japan's Navy Minister from 1906 to 1914), and bears details of the battleship *Ikoma*'s arrival and departure from Singapore in 1910.

Commemorative pictorial postmarks, along with specially produced postcards, were also issued to celebrate visits from Japanese royalty. For instance, Crown Prince Hirohito's visit to Singapore in 1921 (see PC13 in Chapter 1) was accompanied by a flurry of activity; the Singapore Photography Association produced special postcards to mark the occasion. However, unlike the postcards produced in Japan, these did not feature the sea route of the imperial fleet, but rather various industries (PC116) and sights (PC115) in Singapore, lending a local flavour to the commemoration.

PC113
Featuring the Raffles Museum and Library, the message on this postcard notes the arrival of the warship *Ikoma* in Singapore on the morning of 12 October 1910 and its departure on 16 October. While the postcard is dated 15 October, it only reached Marunouchi post office on 31 October. The commemorative ink stamp (top left on front of postcard) features what appears to be a traveller's palm tree with the words "commemoration" and "welcome", and is dated 12 October 1910. The top of the ink stamp reads: "The Imperial Naval Cruiser Ikoma" and "Singapore" at the bottom.
Dated 15 October 1910.
Publisher: Koh & Co., Singapore.
Accession no.: B32413805D_0098

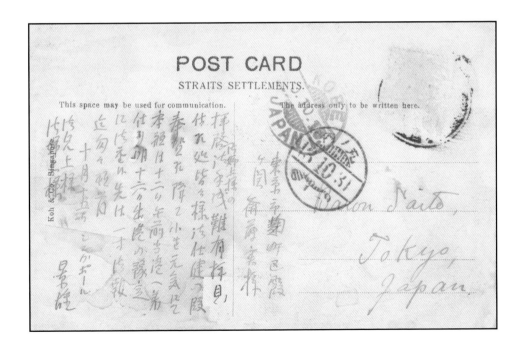

PC114
Featuring the statue of Sir Stamford Raffles, this postcard does not bear a postmark and was likely a collector's item. A handwritten message reads: "Singapore/Sir Stamford Raffles/ Statue" while a commemorative ink stamp reads: "Souvenir of the Long Cruise of the H.I.J.M. (His Imperial Japanese Majesty) Training Squadron 'Adzuma' and 'Sōya'" in Japanese and English, with the words encircling an anchor with two crossed flags. On the left is the flag of Japan, and on the right is the flag of the Imperial Japanese Navy. The training squadron was organised for the Imperial Japanese Naval Officer Cadets in 1912 (Taisho first year).
Date and publisher unknown.
Accession no.: B32413805D_0084

PC115
This postcard featuring scenes of Singapore's coastlines, as well as the iconic Victoria Memorial Hall and clock tower, was also produced by the Japanese community in Singapore in commemoration of the Crown Prince's visit in 1921. Its reverse shows a commemorative stamp dated 18 March 1921 (see facing page), the date of the Crown Prince's arrival in Singapore.
Date unknown. Publisher: Shingapōru Shashin Kyōwa Kai. Accession no.: B32413805D_0122

PC116
This postcard, published by Shingapōru Shashin Kyōwa Kai, was produced by the Japanese community in Singapore in commemoration of the Crown Prince's visit in 1921 (Taisho 10th year). Its reverse bears the same commemorative stamp as the one on PC115. Postcards like PC115 and PC116 were designed to visually relate what Singapore was all about: from its iconic architecture and tropical landscapes, to its industry, local wildlife and waterways. *Date unknown. Publisher: Shingapōru Shashin Kyōwa Kai. Accession no.: B32413805D_0123*

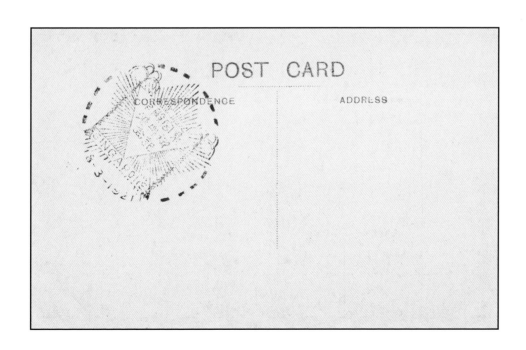

Celebrating Japanese Traditions

Aside from commemorating special visits, postcards were also used by the local Japanese community for another unique reason – the Japanese tradition of sending *nengajō*, or New Year greeting cards, to friends and acquaintances (PC117). Used to express gratitude as well as to keep in touch with friends and relatives overseas, these postcards doubtless took on a special meaning for Japanese living in Singapore. In PC118, the writer, Kaneko (first name illegible), conveys his well wishes on 1 January (year unknown) to an acquaintance living in Nagoya, stressing that it was his first New Year away from Japan.

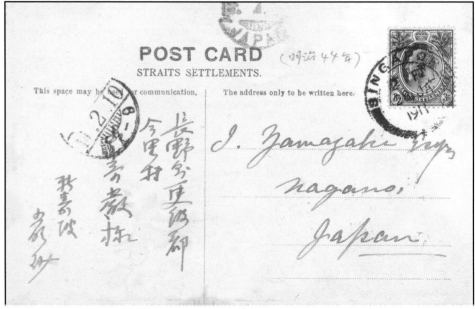

PC117
A New Year card addressed to Mr Yamagaki from Nagano, Japan. This postcard features Indian workmen laying electric cables in Singapore. Written on the front of the postcard is "謹賀新年", which means "Happy New Year" in Japanese.
Postmarked 28 January 1911.
Publisher unknown.
Accession no.: B32413805D_0061

PC118
A New Year Card addressed to S. Tsuboi in Nagoya, this postcard features Kling boys. The term "kling" was derived from the word "Kalinga", the name of an ancient empire in southern India. While acceptable during 19th century Singapore, over time the term "kling" took on a derogatory meaning. *Date and publisher unknown. Accession no.: B32413805D_0109*

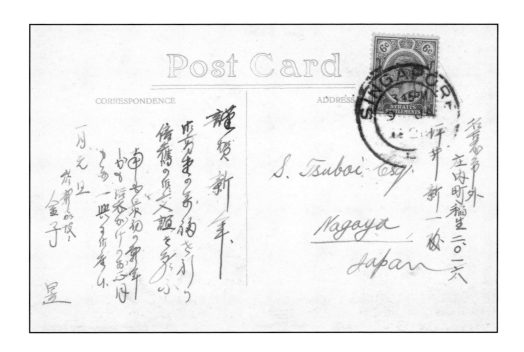

The New Year greeting cards also enabled Japanese communities across Southeast Asia to keep in touch with one another. PC119 was addressed to a Mr Shimaya in Singapore, from a friend living in Melaka. Unlike Kaneko's postcard, this postcard features individuals posing with their pets in front of what appears to be a house. The women are dressed in traditional *kimono*; interestingly, the photo also features a non-Japanese child in *kebaya* (traditional dress worn by women in Indonesia and some parts of Southeast Asia). In contrast, the man in the foreground of the picture, presumably Japanese, dons a shirt with a mandarin collar and Western-style trousers and shoes.

Another New Year card (PC120) was sent from someone living in Singapore to relatives living in Klandasan, Balikpapan, a seaport city on the east coast of Borneo.

Apart from the practice of sending New Year greeting cards, Singapore's Japanese community also observed other occasions, such as *hatsumōde*, the first shrine visit of the year (PC121). Observing familiar cultural traditions in a land far away from home must have mattered greatly to the Japanese community as it would have helped them to stay close to their roots and provide a connection to their families in Japan.

THE "WRONG" TYPE OF POSTCARD

While postcards certainly enabled local Japanese residents to keep in contact with friends and family back home, sending the "wrong" type of postcard could land one in hot soup. For instance, in 1935, Ishihara S., a Japanese electrical salesman, was fined 60 Straits dollars, or three months' imprisonment, for sending "obscene articles" to Japan.

The articles in question were obscene postcards that Ishihara had sent in a parcel to a friend in Nagoya. Unfortunately for Ishihara, they were discovered by postal authorities in Japan and sent back to Singapore, leading to the charges. Whether Ishihara had known about the rules against sending such risqué material overseas is unclear, but what is interesting is that the Japanese postal authorities did not send the rejected parcel back to Ishihara, but instead directed it to the Post Office in Singapore. This suggests that the postal authorities of some countries – or at least that of Japan and Singapore – worked together to prevent the sending and receiving of contraband items.

Source: Obscene postcards – smart fine on Japanese salesman [Microfilm: NL 4049]. (1935, November 20). *Malaya Tribune*, p. 19.

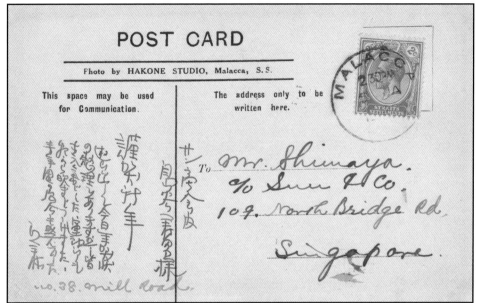

PC119
This *nengajō* (New Year's greeting card), showing individuals dressed in various traditional and modern dress, was addressed to Mr Shimaya at Sun & Co., North Bridge Road in Singapore. The sender's address was 38 Mill Road in Melaka.
Date unclear. Publisher: Hakone Studio, Malacca. Accession no.: B32413805D_0091

PC120
Featuring the Singapore
Cricket Club prior to the
construction of its new
wings, this *nengajō* was sent
by Ōta Sui to relatives living
in Balikpapan, Borneo.
Dated 1 January 1921.
Publisher unknown.
Accession no.:
B32413805D_0088

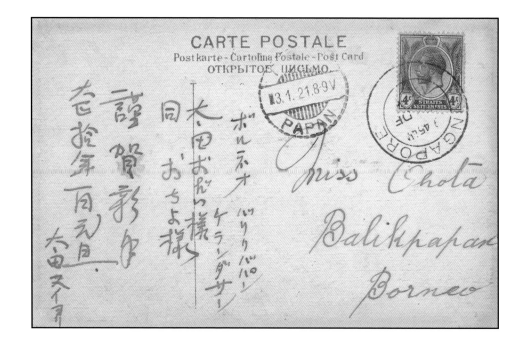

PC121
This postcard, showing an elephant procession, was sent from Taiping, Malaya to Mr Shimaya. In Perak and Kedah, elephant processions such as these occurred during festivals and celebrations. In his message, the writer notes that the first shrine visit of the year was "worse than usual". The postcard arrived in Melaka on 3 January 1921.
Postmarked 1 January 1921 (Singapore). Publisher: Hakone Studio, Malacca. Accession no.: B32413805D_0090

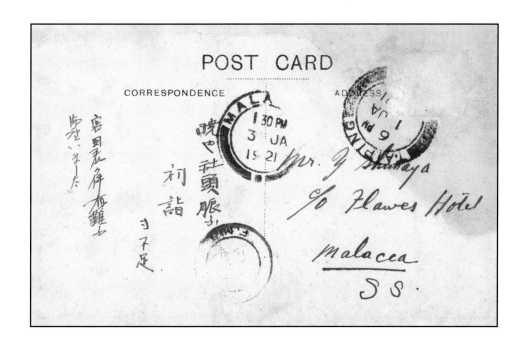

Postcards as Visual Documentation

Postcards were also used as visual documentation by some Japanese. Actual photographs of events, or interesting subjects and landscapes were sometimes made into postcards. Some buyers used the postcard as a means of remembering an event or subject and would jot down notes about the image featured on the postcard. An example is PC122. This postcard was produced by Togo & Co. and bears an image of a tiger. The caption on the reverse of the postcard notes that the tiger featured was found on the Malay peninsula and known to appear frequently in the jungled interiors of Singapore. The insertion of *furigana* text, a reading aid to help with the correct pronunciation of the *kanji* character 馬, also suggests that the writer was keen to ensure the accuracy of his records.

Postcards were also used by individuals to document their observations of the architectural landscape. PC123–126 show buildings along High Street and views of the harbour and Victoria Memorial Hall and Town Hall (now Victoria Theatre and Concert Hall). PC123–125 bear similar handwriting, suggesting that they were probably written by the same individual. According to the notes on PC123, the buildings depicted were a section of those facing the sea in Singapore's uptown. PC124 notes that the image on the postcard was the harbour where ships came to dock. The message on PC125 describes the area around Victoria Memorial Hall and Town Hall.

Postcards were favoured over letters by some people as a medium of communication as the former allowed senders to share interesting scenes of Singapore with their friends, family and acquaintances overseas in a compact and portable format. The only disadvantage perhaps was the lack of space to pen lengthy messages – although for some this would have provided the perfect excuse not to write!

Whether used as a means of personal correspondence, visual documentation, or as a souvenir, it is clear that picture postcards played a crucial role in helping the local Japanese community stay connected with people back home in Japan and throughout the region. Separated across the seas, postcards allowed Japanese immigrants to maintain a sense of their unique identity even as they built new lives in their adopted homes.

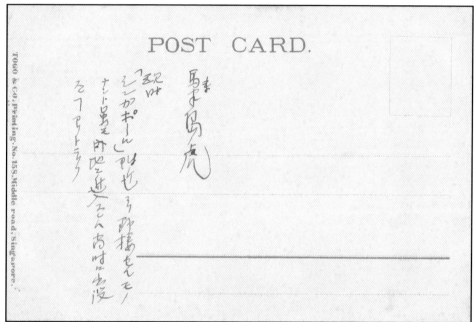

PC122
On the back of this postcard featuring a tiger is a note
explaining that this was a Malayan Tiger and that
they frequently appeared in Singapore. Wild tigers
were not uncommon in 19th-century Singapore; by
the 20th century they had all but disappeared.
Date unknown. Publisher: Togo & Co. Printing.
Accession no.: B32440324K_0013

PC123
Boat Quay, featuring
Guthrie & Co. Ltd in the
background. The company
was one of the biggest rubber
producers in the region, and
one of the chief import-
export agencies between
Britain and Southeast Asia.
The text on the reverse of
the postcard notes that these
are sea-facing buildings in
uptown Singapore.
*Date and publisher
unknown. Accession no.:
B32440324K_0030*

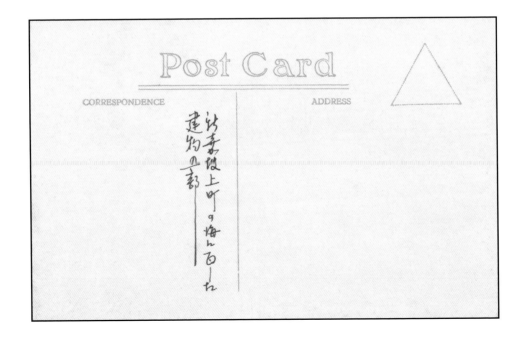

PC124
This postcard features the view of the Singapore waterfront. The notes on the reverse of the postcard states that the pictured location is where ships came to dock. The building on the left is the now demolished Ocean Building.
Date and publisher unknown. Accession no.: B32440324K_0035

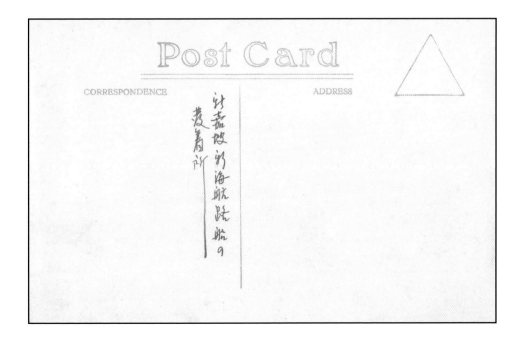

PC125
View of Singapore featuring Victoria Memorial Hall and Town Hall. The note on the back of the postcard reads: "Singapore's clock tower. The pointed roof that can be seen on the opposite side is the [...] Christian temple [likely referring to St Andrew's Cathedral]. The open space is the grounds of the Cricket Club." The new wings of the Singapore Cricket Club had already been built; at the opposite end of the Padang is the Singapore Recreation Club (established in 1883).
Date and publisher unknown. Accession no.: B32440324K_0047

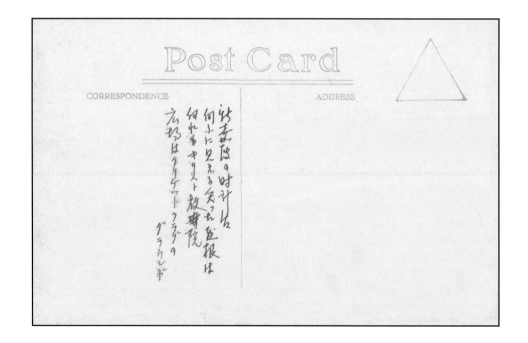

PC126
This postcard features High Street, which was a popular shopping haven. It was also the first street to be laid out in Singapore. This card was part of a series of 12 postcards from a booklet called *Views of Singapore (Series 3)*.
Date unknown.
Publisher: M. S. N. Co.
Accession no.: B34488212J

Notes

1   The Japanese Association. (2016). シンガポール日本人社会百年史：星月夜の耀 [100 Year History of Japanese Community in Singapore (1915–2015)]. Singapore: The Japanese Association, p. 28. (Call no.: RSING 305.895605957 ONE); 伊藤友治郎 [Tomojiro Itō]. (1914). 南洋群嶋寫真畫帳：附南洋事情 [*Nanyō guntō shashin gachō: Fu Nanyō jijō*]. Eiryō Penan Shi: Nanyō chōsakai, p. 21. (Call no.: RRARE 959 ITO)

2   The original Saiyūji Temple was demolished in 1960.

3   The Japanese Association, 2016, p. 52.

4   The Japanese Association, 2016, p. 28.

5   The Japanese Association, 2016, p. 29.

6   The Japanese Association, 2016, p. 82

7   Part of the Lim Shao Bin Collection, the digitised version of 馬来に於ける邦人活動の現况 [Current Status of the Activities of the Japanese in Malaya] is available on BookSG.

8   The Japanese Association, 2016, p. 82; The picture for postcard 111 appears on page 75 of Tsukuda, M. (1917). 馬来に於ける邦人活動の現况 [Current Status of the Activities of the Japanese in Malaya]. Singapore: Nanyō oyobi Nipponjinsha. (Call no.: RRARE 305.89560595 TSU-[LSB]). A digital version is available on BookSG.

9   Lim, S.B. (2004). *Images of Singapore: From the Japanese perspective (1868–1941)*. Singapore: Japanese Cultural Society, p. 148. (Call no.: RSING 959.57 IMA-[HIS])

10   好文館出版部 [Kōbunkan shuppanbu] (Ed.). (1920). 南洋総覧 [Nanyō sōran]. Singapore: Dōshuppanbu, p. 5. (Not available in NLB holdings). "*Nanyō*", which is generally translated as "South Seas", is a vague term with a varied usage over time. It was first mentioned in Shiga Shigetaka's book, *Nanyō,* in 1887. See also Peattie, M. (1988). *Nan'yo: The Rise and Fall of the Japanese in Micronesia*. Honolulu: University of Hawaii Press, pp. xvii – xviii. (Call no. RSEA 996.5 PEA) for a discussion of the term. It is unclear when Singapore first became a part of *Nanyō*, though contemporaries such as Nishimura mention Singapore as part of *Nanyō* from as early as 1902. (Nishimura, 1935, p. 15). For a naval definition of *Nanyō*, see Schencking, J.C. (1999). "The Imperial Japanese Navy and the Constructed Consciousness of a South Seas Destiny, 1872 – 1921" in *Modern Asian Studies* 33(4). London: Cambridge University Press, p. 769. Retrieved from JSTOR via NLB eResources website.

11   Kōbunkan shuppanbu, 1920, p. 51.

12   The Japanese Association, 2016, pp. 61, 64.

13   Cruiser "Kuma" here from Bangkok. [Microfilm: NL 4032]. (1934, February 26). *Malaya Tribune*, p. 11.

14   The Japanese Association, 2016, p. 46.

CARTE POSTALE

Postkarte-Cartolina Postale-Post Card
ОТКРЫТОЕ ПИСЬМО.

SUPPLEMENTARY POSTCARDS

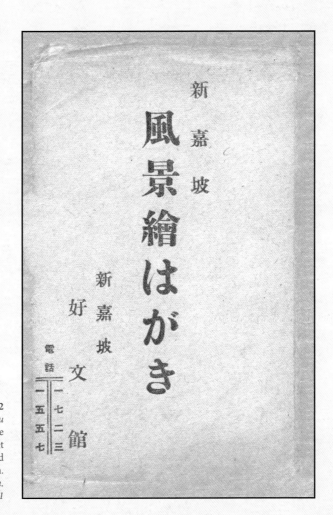

Figure 2
The envelope for *Shingapōru Fukei Ehagaki* (Singapore Landscapes on Postcards), a set of postcards produced by Kōbunkan.
Date and publisher unknown.
Accession no.: B32413805D_0171

PC127
These postcards
(PC127–134) are part of a
set of 20 that were produced
by Kōbunkan.

Located by the Singapore
River, Battery Road was
a trade and commercial
hub, home to godowns
(warehouses), banks and
department stores. On the
left is the Red House, which
housed the Medical Hall. In
the background, partially
obscured by trees, is the
Bank of Taiwan. In front of
the trees is the
Tan Kim Seng fountain.
*Date and publisher
unknown. Accession no.:
B32413805D_0171*

PC128
A view of Raffles Place. The
iconic Red House to the
right of the postcard was
torn down in 1970 to make
way for the Straits Trading
Building.
*Date and publisher
unknown. Accession no.:
B32413805D_0171*

PC129
The Raffles Chambers Building, designed by architectural firm Swan & Maclaren, was completed in 1912. It became the home of the department store, Robinson & Co., in 1941. In 1972, a fire destroyed the building. The site is now occupied by One Raffles Place.
Date and publisher unknown. Accession no.: B32413805D_0171

PC130
Located along Collyer Quay, Johnston Pier was made of iron and wood and comprised a 40-foot-wide platform that extended into the sea. It was completed in 1856 and demolished by 1935.
Date and publisher unknown. Accession no.: B32413805D_0171

PC131
The entrance gate to the Government House (present-day Istana) which served as the residence of the Governor of the Straits Settlements until 1959. Government House was designed by colonial engineer John Frederick Adolphus McNair and built by Indian convict labourers. It was completed in 1869.
Date and publisher unknown. Accession no.: B32413805D_0171

PC132
A view of Stamford Road, named after Sir Stamford Raffles. Running alongside the road was Stamford Canal, which often overflowed its banks at high tide.
Date and publisher unknown. Accession no.: B32413805D_0171

PC133
Anderson Bridge was built between 1908–1910 at the cost of about 450,000 Straits dollars. It was gazetted as a national monument, along with Cavenagh and Elgin bridges, in 2019.
Date and publisher unknown. Accession no.: B32413805D_0171

PC134
A small herd of cattle in a river, possibly the Rochor River that once flowed in the vicinity of Selegie and Rochor Canal roads.
Date and publisher unknown. Accession no.: B32413805D_0171

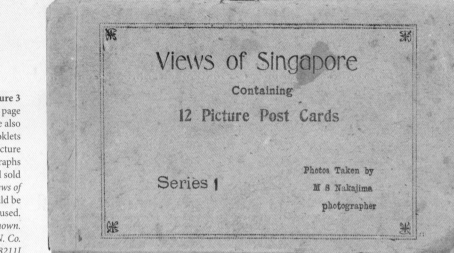

Figure 3
Besides envelopes (see page
173), postcards were also
packaged in small booklets
for sale. This set of 12 picture
postcards features photographs
by M.S. Nakajima and sold
as a booklet called *Views of
Singapore*. Postcards could be
torn out and used.
Date unknown.
Publisher: M.S.N. Co.
Accession no.: B34488211I

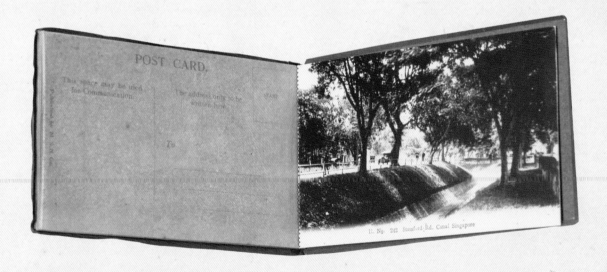

SELECTED POSTCARDS WITH TRIANGLE SPACES

This selection of postcards (PC135–158) all feature a distinctive triangle stamp space (see page 153) on their reverse sides. It is thought that the unusual triangular space for stamps were the distinctive feature of photo cards used by a group of some 50 Japanese photographers and artists in the 1920s.

PC135
A young boy holds up a flying fox, with two others pinned onto a tree trunk.
Date and publisher unknown.
Accession no.: B32440324K_0023

PC136
Written in *kanji* characters at the bottom of the postcard is the description "Bird of Paradise".
Date and publisher unknown.
Accession no.: B32440324K_0024

PC138
Crocodiles have had a long history in Singapore.
One of the earliest accounts of crocodiles on the
island can be found in the autobiographical work,
Hikayat Abdullah (Stories of Abdullah) (1849).
Date and publisher unknown.
Accession no.: B32440324K_0025

PC137
A man poses with an orangutan
which are native to the islands of
Borneo and Sumatra.
Date and publisher unknown.
Accession no.: B32440324K_0026

PC139
A pineapple farm in Singapore.
Pineapples were sometimes grown
as a cash crop alongside rubber.
Singapore was a top world producer
of canned pineapples during the early
20th century.
Date and publisher unknown.
Accession no.: B32440324K_0029

PC140
A Malay man poses with fruits of
a *nangka* (jackfruit) tree.
Date and publisher unknown.
Accession no.: B32440324K_0027

PC141
A green-crested lizard perches on a soursop
fruit. Native to Singapore, this reptilian
creature was commonly seen in the past.
Its numbers have declined over time and is
now mostly found in wooded areas.
Date and publisher unknown.
Accession no.: B32440324K_0028

PC142
Tanamera (Tanah Merah, meaning "red
cliffs" in Malay) was named after the
red clay cliffs that once fronted the sea.
"Tanamera" was also mentioned in early
maps of Singapore. The coastline of the area
was altered following the land reclamation
project in the 1970s.
Date and publisher unknown.
Accession no: B32440324K_0114

Pasir Pejang Singapore

Sunset, Singapore.

PC143
Pasir Panjang (Malay for "long beach" or "sand") was named after a sandy beach that stretched from Batu Berlayar to the junctions of Clementi and West Coast roads. Today, Pasir Panjang is a residential, recreational and industrial area.
Date and publisher unknown.
Accession no.: B32413807F_0008

PC144
Sunsets along coconut tree-lined beaches were popular scenes presented on postcards.
Date and publisher unknown. Accession no.: B32440324K_0033

PC145
Tanjong Katong was a scene commonly
featured on postcards. Nishihara pointed
out that it was famous for its picturesque
view of the moon through the coconut trees
that lined the coast (see Nishihara, p. 142;
Shingapōru Nihonjin Kurabu, p. 186).
Date and publisher unknown.
Accession no.: B32440324K_0111

PC146
A man scales up a coconut tree.
Date and publisher unknown.
Accession no.: B32440324K_0116

PC147
A coconut plantation in
Singapore. The handwritten
message reads: "Ceylon […]
coconut cultivation".
Date and publisher unknown.
Accession no.: B32440324K_0119

PC148
A man rides on a bullock cart in the
suburbs of Singapore. Bullock carts
were eventually phased out with the
advent of mechanised transport and
increasing levels of traffic.
Date and publisher unknown.
Accession no.: B32440324K_0134

PC149
Captioned "Bedok Bridge", this postcard presents a view of the wooden bridge across Sungei Bedok in Tanjong Katong. *Date and publisher unknown. Accession no.: B32413806E_0019*

PC150
Garden at MacRitchie Reservoir. MacRitchie Reservoir was the first water supply system implemented in Singapore and was completed in the 1860s. *Date and publisher unknown. Accession no.: B32440324K_0039*

PC151
A scene along
Connaught Drive, which runs
between today's Esplanade
Park and the Padang.
*Date and publisher
unknown. Accession no.:
B32413806E_0079*

PC152
The Tan Kim Seng fountain
was relocated to Connaught
Drive from Fullerton Square
in 1925. In the background
is the General Post Office.
The handwritten message
reads: "along part of
the waterfront".
*Date and publisher
unknown. Accession no.:
B32413806E_0082*

PC153
A road lined with cotton trees in Jalan Besar. The trees were eventually cut down with the area's urbanisation.
Date and publisher unknown. Accession no.: B32440324K_0037

PC154
Featuring Esplanade in Singapore, this postcard presents Empress Place Building to the left, the Victoria Memorial Hall clock tower in the centre with the Singapore Cricket Club in front of it and Hotel de l' Europe on the right. In the foreground is the Padang, with a gas lamp at its edge.
Date and publisher unknown. Accession no.: B32440324K_0096

PC155
The postcard features Victoria Memorial Hall, Town Hall and clock tower (left), the Dalhousie Obelisk (centre) and St Andrew's Cathedral (right, in background). The new wings of the Singapore Cricket Club on the right had already been built (right, in white) when this image was taken.
Date and publisher unknown. Accession no.: B32440324K_0141

PC156
This picture features the Dalhousie Obelisk (left), the Empress Place Building (presently the Asian Civilisations Museum), and the statue of Raffles (bottom right).
Date and publisher unknown. Accession no.: B32413807F_0019

PC157
Captioned as "Mahammedan Mosque, Singapore", this building is actually the former Nagore Dargah Indian Muslim Shrine at the corner of Telok Ayer and Boon Tat streets. It was gazetted as a national monument in 1974 and in 2011 became the Nagore Dargah Indian Muslim Heritage Centre.
Date and publisher unknown. Accession no.: B32413806E_0124

PC158
The Siong Lim Temple (Lian Shan Shuang Lin Monastery) at Jalan Toa Payoh. It is the oldest Buddhist monastery in Singapore.
Date unknown and publisher unknown. Accession no.: B32413806E_0058

Acknowledgements

This book would not have been possible without the generous help of many people. We would like to express our gratitude to Mr Lim Shao Bin for allowing us to use his extensive collection of postcards, and his generosity in his continued support for the project. The National Library Board must be thanked for their dedication and professionalism in bringing the project to completion. In particular, we would like to mention Tan Huism, Francis Dorai, Wong Siok Muoi, Gracie Lee and Stephanie Pee.

We would like to extend our thanks to Satō Yoshifumi, Deputy Director of the NYK Maritime Museum, Japan, for providing us with the information on NYK shipping routes and passenger numbers. We would also like to thank Yejin Park for her research assistance. Regina and Xi Min, in particular, would like to thank their colleagues in Takikawa City and Mikasa City in Hokkaido, as well as their families for all their encouragement, love and support.

Regina Hong, Ling Xi Min and Naoko Shimazu
Chicago and Singapore, 2020

Police St., Singapore.